Thoughts on Building Strong Towns

Volume II

Charles L. Marohn, Jr.

Daniel Herriges | Nathaniel Hood | Gracen Johnson | Matthias Leyrer | Andrew Price | Rachel Quednau | Johnny Sanphillippo

Foreword by Former Mayor of Seattle, Michael McGinn

Copyright © 2016 Strong Towns

All rights reserved.

ISBN-13: 978-1533018557

DEDICATION

We dedicate this book to the members of our Founding Circle, our original supporters:

Alex Cecchini | Alex Pline | Andrew Burleson | Andrew Price| Ann Pierce | Beckye Frey | Brad Clark | Brad Lonberger | Brian Skeele | Bruce Nesmith | Bruce Wittchen | Catherine Hartley | Charles Marohn | Chris Robbins | Christopher Wilson | Cory Johnston | Dan Allison | Daniel Herriges | Darla Letourneau | Dave Alden | Dave Baur | Derek Hofmann | Don Rice | Edward Erfurt | Edwin W Moore IV | Eric Orozco | Erika Ragsdale | Frank Mansbach | Gracen Johnson | Gregory Jones | Harold (Hank) Weiss | Ian Rasmussen | Isaac Kremer | James Hampson | Jason Wittek | Jeffrey Sleasman | Jesse Bailey | Jim Kumon | John Beaston | John Gear | John Reuter | John Riecke | John Thomas | Jon Korneliussen | Jonathan Hay | Jonathan Mark | Josh Naramore | Julie Black | Justin Burslie | Kerry Hayes | Kevin Shepherd | Kit Anderson | Kristen Jeffers | Lee Myers | Lindsey Meek | Lori Hight | Marielle Brown | Mark E Martin | Mark Gorton | Marta Salij | Matt Taylor | Matthew Steele | Max Mulvihill | Max Siegel | Mike Lydon | Mikel Wilkins | Nate Hood | Padriac Steinschneider | Pat Trahan | Patricia Rosnel | Paul Fritz | Peter Forbes | Phil Jonat | Richard Bose | Rick Smith | Rik Adamski | Ron Beitler | Russell Preston | Ryan Ammann | Scott Biersdorff | Scott Polikov | Seth Zeren | Skyler Yost | Spencer Agnew | Stephen Lassiter | Steve Arnold | Steve Hiniker | Steven Shultis | Susan Horst | Tory Brecht | Warren Rempel

None of this could have happened without their original support.

Strong Towns

CONTENTS

	Acknowledgments	i
	Foreword by Michael McGinn	iii
1.	**Can you be an engineer and speak out for reform?** by Charles Marohn	1
2.	**No New Roads** by Charles Marohn	7
3.	**Dealing with Congestion** by Charles Marohn	15
4.	**The Classic Case** by Charles Marohn	20
5.	**Iowa DOT Chief says the System is Going to Shrink** by Charles Marohn	28
6.	**Suburban Bailout** by Charles Marohn	32
7.	**Slow the Cars** by Charles Marohn	39
8.	**A Statistically Inevitable Outcome** by Charles Marohn	45
9.	**The Fight for Pedestrian Safety** by Nathaniel Hood	54
10.	**Gross Negligence** by Charles Marohn	59
11.	**Dodging Bullets** by Charles Marohn	61
12.	**The Bollard Defense** by Charles Marohn	67
13.	**Just an Accident** by Charles Marohn	74
14.	**Granularity** by Andrew Price	81

15.	**A Strong Towns Response to Homelessness**	96
	by Rachel Quednau	
16.	**The Five Ways Engineers Deflect Criticism**	101
	by Charles Marohn	
17.	**The Least Dumb Idea that Consensus Provides**	109
	by Charles Marohn	
18.	**Middle of the Road Kentucky**	114
	by Johnny Sanphillippo	
19.	**Moving the Overton Window**	121
	by Daniel Herriges	
20.	**My Car Pays Cheaper Rent Than Me**	133
	by Andrew Price	
21.	**I'm Not Afraid**	139
	by Charles Marohn	
22.	**The Density Question**	145
	by Charles Marohn	
23.	**Efficiency**	151
	by Charles Marohn and Ruben Anderson	
24.	**What the World Needs Now**	156
	by Gracen Johnson	
25.	**Too Wild to Imagine**	161
	by Charles Marohn	
	Glossary	167
	About the Authors	171
	About Strong Towns	175
	Endnotes	176

ACKNOWLEDGMENTS

Everyone who writes for Strong Towns once did so as a volunteer. Most remain in that capacity still. The only compensation they receive for their efforts comes from within; the satisfaction they get from creating, the hope that their contribution can move the world forward in a positive way.

Anyone who has ever seriously exposed their thoughts to the broad marketplace of ideas knows a feeling of vulnerability. We want to start this book by thanking all of the Strong Towns contributors, and all those who have shared our message with others, for their willingness to step out from the crowd.

FOREWORD
by Michael McGinn

When I moved to my neighborhood of Greenwood in 1999, I started working to get sidewalks. Annexed by Seattle in the 1950's, it was built before sidewalks were required. And I kept hearing the strangest thing from our Department of Transportation: "We can't afford to build sidewalks. We don't even have the money to take care of our arterials and bridges."

That didn't seem right to me. Seattle had difficulties, but on the whole it was a successful city hosting many very profitable companies. Surely there was money available for something as basic as sidewalks. Particularly since Greenwood was an "urban village," Seattle's term for places with neighborhood businesses, bus lines, and apartment buildings that were slated to take the most growth.

So I set off to get some money for my neighborhood, as well as figure out where the money was going. Neighborhood meetings led to city stakeholder groups, which then led to ballot measure fights as well as starting my own non-profit to advocate for urban sustainability. Which then lead to me winning a race to be Mayor of Seattle.

As crazy as the trip was, what's even crazier is that the DOT folks were right. There *wasn't* enough money. The state and federal government were wasting billions on highway expansion, including an ill-fated highway tunnel under Seattle's downtown. But the problem was deeper than just waste or a bad highway or two. Our patterns of land use and development made no sense environmentally, socially or financially. Politics rewarded megaprojects, even though more granular investments would generate more jobs, more safety, and better quality of life per dollar spent. There was something fundamentally wrong.

Somewhere in this journey I came across a little website called StrongTowns.org, where a civil engineer named Chuck Marohn had abandoned his career to dissect and understand the problem. He was describing exactly what I had experienced; we created places that could not financially sustain themselves. And we agreed on the prescription—a return to the traditional ways of building places that allowed regular people a shot at the good life.

What made him even more interesting to me was that he was obviously pretty conservative politically, and I definitely come from the progressive end of the spectrum. When I got him on my podcast he admitted he used to be a Republican but now says, "I don't really fit into the political spectrum." He then added, "And you're kind of an oddball too!"

It's hard to look at our nation's deepening economic and social divisions and feel like the political parties have this right. I have my strong preference, but both are too beholden to powerful economic actors that use the process to benefit themselves, at a staggering cost to the rest of us.

I was invited to speak at Strong Towns' first National Gathering in 2014, where I met many of the authors in the volume to follow. For me, it was a hopeful moment.

Unburdened by ideology, these Strong Citizens were talking about how they could work at the local level to improve the places where they lived.

It's a different way. From the bottom up, not the top down. Where people are individuals, not "the other side." And which gives us a pathway out of the mess we've created.

So what exactly is the Strong Towns movement? Well, part of its beauty is that if you like it, you get to help define it by your own actions. I invite you to read on with an open mind, and then take action in your own community. You never know where it will take you. If you do, you'll meet some great people, and you'll make your place a little better. And most of all, you can help contribute to a new way of thinking about our places that will help build a better future.

1. CAN YOU BE AN ENGINEER AND SPEAK OUT FOR REFORM?
by Charles Marohn

(February 4, 2015) Last week, I received a notice from the board of licensing that a complaint had been filed against my professional engineering license. The complaint indicated that I had engaged in "misconduct on the website/blog Strong Towns" for things I had written critical of the engineering profession. While this development is disappointing, it is far from surprising.

The complaint was filed by a former American Society of Civil Engineers fellow who is currently an outspoken member of the Move MN coalition, the organization advocating for more transportation funding in my home state. The complaint was filed on the day I wrote "No New Roads" an essay that called out both organizations for their self-serving support of endless transportation spending (see Chapter 2). Again, an effort to take away my professional license for speaking out is appalling, but it isn't surprising.

I've long opposed the American Society of Civil Engineers.[i] They don't represent me and they should not be allowed to speak for the profession unchallenged. Their stands on how our country should be developed are frequently cited as standard, despite how stunningly radical they are.[ii] American prosperity is not simply a function of how many roads, pipes and hunks of metal we can construct. Our infrastructure investments must work to support the American people, not the other way around.

I've also been an outspoken critic of the Move MN coalition and its version of success (see Chapter 4). I've had professional colleagues suggest to me that I'm on the wrong side here, that a more lucrative path for me and for Strong Towns would be to get on board and advocate for more taxpayer money to expand the current system. I've been told privately that I'm not a "real engineer" if I don't support more funding. That's just wrong.

Most importantly, I've been critical of how the engineering profession approaches safety within our cities.[iii] I coined the word "stroad" to describe the industry's standard approach of over-engineering America's urban and suburban streets as if they were high speed, high-capacity roads. The current variant of the engineering profession gained prominence in the era of highway building, but that knowledge set does not apply to complex places where people exist outside of automobiles. (See Section II, Slow the Cars, for more on this subject.) It is *malpractice* to suggest otherwise, a term I will not back down from using.

Our urban streets need to be safe for everyone, whether in a car, on a bike, in a wheelchair or simply walking.[iv] Today they are not and that is unacceptable.

Should I be allowed to be an engineer? Can a licensed engineer oppose new road construction and still retain his license? Can a licensed engineer question the appalling safety record resulting from standard industry practices and be allowed to remain in the industry?

A review of Minnesota law raises some doubt. Here's what Minnesota Rule 1805.0200 requires for the personal conduct of licensed engineers:

> *A licensee shall avoid any act which may diminish public confidence in the profession and shall, at all times, conduct himself or herself, in all relations with clients and the public, so as to maintain its reputation for professional integrity.*

Now who is such language designed to protect? Does it protect society at large or does it protect the engineering firms who have thrown their weight behind efforts to secure more funding at the State Capitol? Does it protect the vulnerable or does it protect the engineer who simply signs the plans, confident that the standards will shield them from liability, regardless of the outcome?[v]

I'm not going to let this intimidation change what I do. It has strengthened my resolve to stand up, be heard and lead this movement in building a nation of strong towns.

The engineering profession is full of great people working to do good things, but it also has a pervasive dark element within it. There are many who are way too comfortable with the power that comes from having a large budget, access to influential people and the protection of industry standards. Contracts written as a percent of construction costs, feasibility studies that ignore the second life cycle and fraudulent benefit/cost analyses are accepted byproducts of this destructive mindset.[vi] I've spoken out against all of them and will continue to do so.

All truth goes through three stages. First, it is ridiculed. Second, it is violently opposed. Third, it is accepted as being self-evident. I've been telling the Strong Towns board and staff for the past year to be prepared, we are entering the second stage. The good news is that I can see the third stage on the horizon and it is approaching fast.

I've spoken with college classes at engineering schools around the country. These students are not encumbered by the profession's dogma. They live the problems we talk about at Strong Towns and want to do things differently when they get their licenses. When I've shown our video, *Conversation with an Engineer*, to groups of professionals, I've watched many of the old, stodgy engineers sit straight-faced with arms crossed while the younger crowd laughs and gives high-fives to each other.[vii] Have faith; change is coming.

I regularly have engineers email me to say they support what we're doing but are afraid to speak up for fear of how it might impact their career. There's strength in numbers. Now's the time to join the movement, let people know this conversation needs to happen and volunteer to be part of reshaping the engineering profession — and our cities — for the next generation.

This time the licensing board found "no violation" and so, fortunately, no further action is pending. This time. I've been warned that my file could be reopened "should additional evidence warrant" doing so. Let's hope that we don't have to face that, that further threats like this aren't an ongoing part of the opposition playbook.

Thank you for your support and for doing what you can to make yours a strong town.

Section I: No New Roads

2. NO NEW ROADS
by Charles Marohn

For years, we have worked to draw attention to the problems of excessive road building. Not only are nearly all expansion projects losing investments themselves – we are far past the point of diminishing returns – but they are distorting our economy in unhealthy ways, destroying local businesses, bankrupting our cities and making our neighborhoods less safe.

These are all complex, nuanced insights that run counter to the prevailing cultural wisdom of America, the common belief that simply equates new road building with growth and then growth with prosperity. At Strong Towns, we finally just made it simple: No New Roads.

Let's stop building new roads when we have no idea – not even the faintest notion – of how we are going to pay to maintain the ones we've already built. As Tennessee Transportation Commissioner John Schroer said, "You don't build an addition on to your house when you can't afford to fix the leaking roof."

No New Roads is not *never* new roads. We understand that there are places where investments need to be made, but as you'll see in the following set of articles, American transportation policy is about expansion first, second and third with the actual work of maintaining – let alone making better use of what we've already built – a distant afterthought.

When you see the hashtag #NoNewRoads, you are seeing a plea for sanity.

* * * * *

(January 5, 2015) Minnesota's legislative session begins tomorrow and, like many states throughout the union, front and center on the agenda is transportation spending. From this weekend's edition of the state's newspaper of record, the Star Tribune[viii]:

> *Anybody who travels around the state knows our highways are in worse condition, our traffic congestion is getting worse, public transit is far behind other parts of the country and world in terms of its adequacy and efficiency," [Minnesota Governor Mark] Dayton said in an interview. "I can guarantee that if we don't make it better, it's going to continue to get worse.*

Making it "better" means, of course, spending more money. There is no talk of reform. There is nobody really asking how we got in such a difficult financial situation. The only question under consideration is the one I outlined in my book, *A World Class Transportation System*: How do we get more money to continue doing more of the same thing?

More is better.

The Star Tribune reported that, "about 1,200 of Minnesota's more than 20,000 bridges are classified as structurally deficient."[ix] They attributed Transportation for America later in naming the exact number: 1,191. The 2013 Transportation for America bridge report[x] was an update of a 2011 report on the same topic. While the 2013 update didn't include the cost of repairs, the 2011 report did.

Transportation for America indicated in 2011 that the cost to repair Minnesota's structurally-deficient bridges was $500 million.[xi] That's a lot of money, but these bridges also accommodate a combined 2.3 million crossings per day.

Contrast that with the new bridge being constructed over the St. Croix River. At a final cost estimated to be somewhere around $600 million, it will carry a projected 16,000 cars per day.[xii]

Maintain 1,191 existing bridges: $500 million. Build one new bridge: $600 million. The former is a crisis while the latter is destiny.

The St. Croix bridge is just one specific example. The Star Tribune story points out that the majority of what we are spending goes to expansion. Keep in mind that the problem we are being told we have is insufficient money to maintain everything we have built. As our state's version of a transportation advocacy organization, Move MN, has said, we are the "Land of 10 million potholes".[xiii]

Well, here's how we prioritize maintenance: Minnesota's total transportation budget for 2013 was $1.9 billion. Of that $700 million was spent on maintenance and $1.1 billion on new construction. In addition, the federal government provided $721 million for Minnesota roads in 2013.[xiv]

Note that this new construction is not new transit or pedestrian improvements; it's good old road spending. And also note that a large percentage of that $721 million from the federal government is also going to new construction. We can't maintain all the stuff we've built – according to the Star Tribune, Minnesota has the "fifth-largest highway system in the nation" – yet we are building more and more and more.

Let me give you just one example out of a nearly infinite list: the new interchange on Highway 10 at Rice.

Rice, MN has a population of 1,320. They have a highway intersection east of town where they were able to land a pair of gas stations, one with a combination McDonalds/Subway. Last year MnDOT estimated that 3,400 cars per day approach the highway from the west, just 1,600 from the east. The McDonalds business model requires them to be on the northbound side to get those traffic counts which, unfortunately, is the opposite side of the highway from the city. The new interchange will make that easier for everyone, at a cost of only $11.3 million.

Incidentally, these improvements were funded out of the Safety and Mobility Interchange Program, a program designed to "relieve growing traffic congestion" and "promote traffic safety". Inexplicably, construction of this new high-capacity interchange didn't require Rice to abandon either of its other two dangerous highway accesses. For everyone involved, those are future potential economic development opportunities where the state can look forward to subsidizing another international franchise corporation with a future interchange (once enough people have been killed trying to cross there).

This is our system: one big Ponzi scheme attempting to prop up a rolling development extravaganza of strip malls, big box stores, fast food and cheap residential housing. You want to spend more on this?

Sunday's Star Tribune indicated that current funding levels put us "$21.2 billion short" of what is needed "just to keep Minnesota's current system functioning, never mind expanding it." How about we just try that for a while? What would it actually mean to just to keep our current system functioning? What would it mean to try and get more out of our current investments before we expanded the system?

It can't happen, at least not easily, and here's why: It would mean a change in our land use pattern. It would mean a change in tax codes. It would mean a change in our economic development approach. You see, to get more out of our current investments, we need a development pattern that can mature in place, one that doesn't rely on an ever-expanding transportation system to create new fast food, big box and tract housing opportunities. That's a multi-dimensional conversation, one that can't – or at least won't – happen exclusively at the state or federal level.

The nation's transportation funding conversation is happening in a silo. The Star Tribune perfectly summarized the simplicity of that dialog:

> *That coalition's [Move MN] roster of local governments, labor unions, and construction and engineering firms backs new taxes to pay for transportation. But while advocates argue that declining infrastructure hobbles economic growth, many businesses are reluctant to back tax increases that would hit their balance sheets.*[xv]

So who's not represented in that silo? You. Your community. Your small business owners trying to make a go of it on Main Street. The family trying to save money by biking or walking to work. The student wanting competent bus service near her school.

Oh, they'll pander to you. They'll promise you all kinds of things....fancy new trains (to park and rides), bike trails (in the ditch, not on the street)....but this system isn't representing you at all. It's on autopilot. It's got a long line of Rice interchanges and St. Croix bridge projects just ready to go when you give them the money. Don't do it.

I'm going to aggressively oppose any increase in transportation funding in Minnesota, any other state or at the federal level, until there is serious reform of this system. At this point, communal funds must be for maintenance only with any system expansion being paid by some form of user charge.

And if this means that states and the federal government, unable to resolve the complexities of successfully growing a centralized economy without the opiate of transportation spending, devolve funding to the local level for all but the critical systems of interstate travel, then that works too.

As a final word, for those of you hoping to fund transit, pedestrian and cycling improvements out of increased state and federal dollars, I offer two observations. First, you are advocating for high-return investments in a financing system that does not currently value return-on-investment. You are going to finish way behind on every race, at least until we no longer have the funds to even run a race. Stop selling out for a drop in the bucket and start demanding high ROI spending.

Second, the cost of getting anything you want is going to be expansive funding to prop up the systems that hurt the viability of transit, biking and walking improvements. Every dollar you get is going to be bought with dozens of dollars for suburban commuters, their parking lots and drive-thrus, and their mindset continuing to oppose your efforts at every turn. You win more by defunding them than by eating their table scraps.

#NoNewRoads

Strong Towns

THE ONLY THING WORSE THAN HAVING CONGESTION IS NOT HAVING CONGESTION

3. DEALING WITH CONGESTION
by Charles Marohn

(October 19, 2015) Last week, Chris Murphy, a US Senator from Connecticut, took on the issue of transportation. He kicked off the conversation by focusing on the commute and invited people to share their ideas for how to fix it. He even live streamed his ride,[xvi] sharing in the frustration of many who find themselves stuck in crippling traffic each rush hour:

> @ChrisMurphyCT: "I want to know what I can do to help fix your commute. This needs to an honest discussion. Share your story using #FedUp

We became aware of all of this because the Tri-State Transportation Campaign (@Tri-State) copied us on a couple of their responses. To that end, I seem to have been credited in a number of places with the quote: "*Curing congestion by adding more lanes is like curing obesity by buying bigger pants.*" I'm sure I've used that — it's a brilliant line — but you can't credit me with it; these insights on congestion have, sadly, been with us since the early days of highway building.

Sadly, while Senator Murphy calls for an "honest discussion," his argument included this patently false statement right out of the Infrastructure Cult's talking points memo:

> *@ChrisMurphyCT: We're running our transportation system on the same amt of money as 1993. That's not going to help us with the big projects we need #FedUp*

Federal gas tax receipts in 1993 were $19.6 billion.[xvii] By 2013, that had climbed to $29.2 billion. To this, Congress annually adds billions more. Sure, the gas tax has not been increased since 1993, but let's not pretend that is the fundamental cause of our transportation woes or — more importantly — that what we "need" is more "big projects".[xviii]

Most of Senator Murphy's conversation dealt with the chronic issue of congestion. Notice I did not call congestion a problem. It's clearly not. Within our places — on our streets — congestion is an indicator of success.[xix] As Yogi Berra reportedly said: "Nobody goes there any more because it is too busy."

Indeed. The most successful places are full of congestion.

Between our places — on our roads — congestion signals many things but, for me anyway, it primarily indicates America's cultural — and the engineering profession's technical — misunderstanding of the systems we have built.

Consider the hierarchical road network. It's so commonplace today that we rarely stop to question it. Small, local streets empty into collector streets. Those collectors empty into arterials. The arterials empty into major arterials which eventually end up pouring into our highway systems. Small to big; it's the way things are done.

Stop a moment to examine a watershed. There you have ditches that flow into small creeks. Those creeks flow into larger brooks and streams. In turn these flow into larger rivers and, ultimately, these systems come together to form some of the world's major waterways.

We all intuitively understand that, when we experience rain or snow melt on the edges of a watershed, there is a compounding effect that occurs. We've become fairly competent at realizing that, by the time all this rain comes together, it very often produces a flood.

We've so grasped this concept that we've taken steps to address the problem at the source. We don't allow people to fill their wetlands. We require developers to retain their runoff on site. We build retention systems to hold back storm water and feed it into the natural systems more slowly so that flooding does not occur. We take these steps and others *at the source* to mitigate the cumulative, negative impacts of storm water runoff, namely flooding

Instead of a river network, examine a similar system of roadways during a typical commute. Here we have rain of a different sort: the automobiles that emanate forth from the development we induce, subsidize and cheer for out on the periphery of our cities.

Why are we so shocked when this produces a flood? We create the flood.

If we were going to design a system to generate the maximum amount of congestion each day, this is exactly how it would be done. This is why all American cities — big, small and in between — experience some level of congestion during commutes. We take whatever cars we have and funnel them into the same place at the same time. We manufacture a flood.

I've written a short eBook (*A World Class Transportation System*) describing the ways I would go about using price signals to make some rational choices about our transportation investments. I'm going to simplify by sticking with the river analogy. When we want to decrease flooding in a watershed, we go to the source. We try to retain that water, to absorb it as near to where it originates as possible. We understand this is way cheaper and vastly more effective than building massive infrastructure systems to handle the runoff once it is sent downstream.

For automobile flooding (congestion), the only way to deal with it and still have a successful economy is to address it at the source. We need to absorb those trips locally before they become a flood. Instead of building lanes, we need to be building corner stores. We need local economic ecosystems that create jobs, opportunities and destinations for people as an alternative to those they can only get to by driving.

For nearly seven decades, our national transportation obsession has been about maximizing the amount that you *can* drive. We now need to focus on minimizing the amount you are *forced* to drive. If we develop a system that responds to congestion by creating local options, we will not only waste less money on transportation projects that accomplish little but we will be strengthening the finances of our cities. We can spend way less and get back way more.

That's the essence of a Strong Towns approach.

#NoNewRoads

4. THE CLASSIC CASE
by Charles Marohn

(January 19, 2015) On January 16, 2015, Minnesota Public Radio hosted a roundtable discussion on transportation policy.[xx] Featured in the conversation was Margaret Donahue, Executive Director of the Transportation Alliance, the group spearheading the Move MN coalition calling for additional transportation funding.

When discussing the economic benefits of modern transportation spending, Donahue cited three examples: the Green Line light rail transit project in Minneapolis and St. Paul, Highway 212 improvements and the following:

> *You look at [Highway] 371 through Baxter as a classic case. It used to be a sleepy little town and now there's just business after business after business.*[xxi]

Baxter, MN just happens to be the city I grew up in and where I worked as an engineer for a number of years. I totally agree: it is a classic case of what our transportation investments get us. Where I disagree with Donahue, as well as the insiders and vested-interests that comprise the bulk of her coalition, is that this is a positive example.

Baxter is the typical American Ponzi scheme city. From my office window, I watched the 371 bypass of Brainerd be built in the late 1990's. On my desk were a number of projects that today comprise the "business after business..." that constitute this corridor. It will look sadly familiar to where you live, I'm certain.

BUSINESS AFTER BUSINESS AFTER BUSINESS....

If you support the Move MN proposal for additional transportation spending (or similar proposals being floated around the country), here's what success looks like: Super Walmart. JC Penny's. Home Depot. Costco. Kohl's. Mills Fleet Farm. Cub Foods. Gander Mountain. Super 1. Target. Best Buy. Office Max. Menard's. Arby's. Culver's. Taco Bell. The Olive Garden. Buffalo Wild Wings. Kentucky Fried Chicken. Pizza Ranch. Bonanza Family Restaurant. Subway. Starbucks. Applebee's. Cherry Berry. NAPA Auto Parts. NTB Service Station. Super 8. AmericInn. Comfort Suites. Holiday Inn. Two Holiday gas stations. Two Super America gas stations. Multiple car dealerships. A number of banks. And a collection of miscellaneous bets, big and small, tied to the success of these national and regional chains.

Yes, Baxter used to be a sleepy little town. The construction of the Brainerd bypass through Baxter made millionaires out of a handful of lucky bumpkins whose ancestors homesteaded the chosen pieces of woods and swamp a century ago. This paved the way for the predictable collection of national chains that our transportation investments are designed to subsidize.

"Success" in our current transportation funding system means more of this. (Photo of Baxter's Highway 371 strip.)

And while the former owner of the now-failed local grocery store can become the night manager at Walmart (true story), the former owner of the now-failed downtown shoe store can sell shoes at Kohls and the former owner of the now-failed downtown pizza place can run the lunch crew at Applebees', only a handful of people are really benefiting from this arrangement.

This collection of businesses is not making the people of Baxter wealthy. Quite the opposite—it is sucking wealth out of the community, and limiting jobs and opportunity in the process. The wealth needed to compete in this government-led economy is out of reach for almost all Americans. It's a system set up to make the wealthy wealthier. In return, the unwashed masses get cheap imported stuff and fast food.

The city of Baxter does get more than that, however. The local government got a generation of robust growth, a period of time where cash was plentiful, stuff was shiny and new, and everyone involved (including me, to a degree) looked like a genius as a result. That time has passed and Baxter now finds itself in the second phase of the suburban Ponzi scheme: the hanging-on phase. Taxes are going up, debt is increasing and the old way of doing projects is getting harder and harder to pull off. It's becoming really difficult to maintain all this stuff without new growth providing easy cash; there just isn't enough tax base and what's there just isn't financially productive enough.

Of course, the next phase is decline, when deferred maintenance and accumulated debt gives the city few alternatives for responding when these chains start to fail or move on to a shinier and better place. Detroit is future. Ferguson is future. Those places once thought they had it figured out as well, that massive transportation investments would bring them continual prosperity. They were responding to short-term incentives, just like we are here.

THE SLEEPY LITTLE TOWN

The neighboring city of Brainerd is now the sleepy little town. This is where Highway 371 used to run and Brainerd — like thousands of cities around the country — once saw highway-oriented development as its salvation.

That hasn't worked out so well. Those places on the edge of town are now the ones in steep decline, with high long-term vacancy rates and rapidly falling property values.[xxii] In contrast, the core neighborhoods of Brainerd and its downtown — the areas built before our auto experiment — are holding their value, despite disinvestment and decades of neglect from the city. And despite the state dramatically tilting the economic playing field away from Brainerd's small business ecosystem and towards the national chain corridor of Baxter.

If this seems counter-intuitive to you, there is a reason for that. As Ms. Donahue has suggested, we've come to associate transportation improvements with success. We've mistaken the shiny-and-new for the resilient-and-timeless. This is the story of America post-World War II, and it's why our cities are struggling to find the money to do simple things, despite all of America's growth and wealth. Our transportation investments destroy far more community wealth than they create.

GOOD POLITICS. BAD POLICY.

So why would a transportation advocacy group be pushing for billions in new spending on transportation projects that have such low financial returns? Why would such a group want to make investments that dramatically weaken our core cities? Why would those deeply involved in transportation policy not be pushing for dramatic reform of this system before giving it the steroid of a major cash infusion?

There are two simple explanations. First, look at the members of the coalition. The Gold and Silver sponsors of the Transportation Alliance[xxiii] are primarily a collection of the nation's largest engineering firms, major companies that directly benefit from this government spending. The Move MN coalition is broader but is still dominated by contractors, labor unions and those that stand to directly profit from an expansion of the status quo.

The second explanation is that this is good politics. Despite the underlying reality, most Americans do associate shiny-and-new with success. Transportation projects provide an immediate feedback that we're conditioned to interpret as progress. An opaque tax on wholesale gasoline is the least noticeable way to continue to provide what I've called the modern equivalent of Rome's bread and circuses.[xxiv]

QUESTIONS FOR THE UNWASHED MASSES

If you are passionate about major urban areas, why would you want to spend more money on a system designed to take the wealth of cities and direct it to pork-barrel projects in rural areas? Why wouldn't you just keep your money in the city and spend it on your own priorities?

If you are passionate about small businesses, why would you want to continue to subsidize large corporations and national chains and, in the process, create enormous financial barriers for small business success?

If you are a bike/walk advocate, why do you have any confidence that the DOT has even the slightest comprehension of your needs? Why would you agree to partake in the table scraps of a system that considers unwalkable places its greatest successes?

If you are passionate about transit, why would you not opt to fund great transit systems in your own places with your own money instead of sending all that money elsewhere for more highway strip development and then get suburban-commuter rail in exchange?

If you are passionate about the environment or climate change, why would you support an approach that is going to continue to expand an already bloated, auto-oriented system as a precondition to anything else?

If you are a fiscal conservative, how can you support a tax increase — or even worse, more borrowing — for a system that is so financially unproductive and is captured by insider interests?

If you care about social justice, how can you be complicit in building more and more places that are designed to fail, to trap our most vulnerable in decline?

If you are a member of a trade union, do you not see how the franchisement of America has denuded your ranks to the lowest levels since the suburban experiment began?[xxv] Are you for the worker or, as your critics would assert, do you simply advance your own narrow interests at the expense of society?

CONCLUSION

Perhaps the most revealing, albeit disturbing, part of the MPR interview came when the conversation had turned to exactly how much money was needed. This has been a source of dispute because MnDOT has released many different numbers, each time getting further from reality and closer to the politically expedient. Here's what Ms. Donahue had to say on the matter:

> *We can study it to death. Is it $6 billion or $6.2 billion or is it $4 billion or $4.5 billion? The bottom line is, it's a big number and we're going to have to do a lot of work to even get close to those numbers. So instead of wasting time arguing about exactly what the number is maybe we should spend some more time actually getting projects built.*[xxvi]

Our goal should not be to "get projects built" but to have a transportation funding system that makes our people, cities, states and country stronger. While I agree that new transportation funding is needed, new funding without significant reform is worse than no funding at all. We need to continue to oppose all of these funding efforts until serious reform is on the table.

#NoNewRoads

- Does Not

- Creates Jobs
- Spends Money
- Makes a Place

STRONG TOWNS

Want Growth? Get People.

5. IOWA DOT CHIEF SAYS THE SYSTEM IS GOING TO SHRINK
by Charles Marohn

We were involved in breaking some news when I was invited to speak about transportation at a Urban Land institute event in Des Moines. During the Q&A portion, my fellow presenter, Iowa DOT Director Paul Trombino, said something I've been waiting to hear a DOT director say. He said our transportation system is going to shrink.

I gave him an opportunity back away from that and, to his credit, he didn't. When we shared that revelation on our website, along with the audio from the event, it made news widely in transportation circles as well as in Iowa. Again, to his credit, Trombino has continued to speak consistently about the transportation challenges Iowa faces. This is really important.

We have overbuilt our transportation systems. Worse yet, the way we finance transportation encourages states to build even more while neglecting those systems they have already built. Trombino's leadership on this issue brings Iowa a lot closer to asking the next great transportation question: How do we make better use of the systems we've already built?

* * * * *

(July 6, 2015) Last week I spoke at a ULI event in Iowa along with Paul Trombino, the director of the Iowa Department of Transportation. During the Q&A, I was absolutely stunned by something the director said about the state's highway system: *And so the reality is, the system is going to shrink.*[xxvii]

Now I'm stunned not because of what was said — we've been saying the same thing for years — but because of who said it. While I've had a couple say this in private, talk of contraction is not something I've heard any other DOT director share in public. This is a big deal.

Here's specifically what he said:

> *I said the numbers before. 114,000 lane miles, 25,000 bridges, 4,000 miles of rail. I said this a lot in my conversation when we were talking about fuel tax increases. It's not affordable. Nobody's going to pay.*
>
> *We are. We're the ones. Look in the mirror. We're not going to pay to rebuild that entire system.*
>
> *And my personal belief is that the entire system is unneeded. And so the reality is, the system is going to shrink.*
>
> *There's nothing I have to do. Bridges close themselves. Roads deteriorate and go away. That's what happens.*

And reality is, for us, let's not let the system degrade and then we're left with sort of, whatever's left. Let's try to make a conscious choice – it's not going to be perfect, I would agree it's going to be complex and messy – but let's figure out which ones we really want to keep.

And quite honestly, it's not everything that we have, which means some changes.[xxviii]

Director Trombino seems like a decent guy who is speaking honestly with people in a Midwestern fashion I appreciate. I made sure he was comfortable with me quoting him on this before we left the event and he made it clear that he was. That's great because this is a game-changing acknowledgement that every state DOT director should be putting into the public realm.

And I'm going to call it an *acknowledgement*. Most DOT directors understand that we've overbuilt, that there will never be the money to maintain everything they are asked to maintain. And yet, I've not heard another DOT chief admit this problem publicly. They need to.

Here's why: The day after the ULI event, I spoke to a metropolitan planning organization in Cedar Rapids, Iowa. I shared the quote from Trombino with them. Their response: Wish we had known that before because we never would have recommended building more stuff.

Trombino's assessment was both intelligent and pragmatic. Essentially, we can let things fall apart and be left with whatever survives, or we can be more intentional and likely have a far better outcome. That's a rational response, a real Strong Towns approach. We're all in.

In 2009, Iowa had 114,347 highway miles.[xxix] That is one mile for every 27 people. By comparison, Texas — the DOT I've long thought was the most hopelessly over-committed financially — has 87 people per mile. California is 226. So perhaps it is fitting that this acknowledgement first comes from Iowa.

Which state is going to be next? There are 49 more that need to take this first step. Let's try and get them all to speak this honestly.

#NoNewRoads

6. SUBURBAN BAILOUT
by Charles Marohn

(November 2, 2015) A few years ago I was attending a city council meeting where the agenda included a request for the city to take over a private road. The proposal had a positive recommendation from the staff and, of course, the city's engineering consultant, because the property owners agreed to pay the costs (including the engineer's fees) of bringing the road up to city standards. As one of the city council members remarked: "You mean we get a free road?"

Free, indeed.

Of course, the property owners on this dead-end cul-de-sac were not gifting the city a "free road" out of generosity. They wanted something in return. It was their expectation that the city would now assume the long term maintenance obligation associated with their roadway. Not only would the city plow the snow and mow the ditches but it would also — at least in theory — be responsible for sealing the cracks, filling the potholes and, someday, rebuilding the roadway when it fell apart.

And when I pointed out — in a detailed memo with an attached spreadsheet showing my calculations — that the amount of taxes the property owners would pay between the time the city took over that road and the time they would need to make good on their obligation to fix it would amount to less than 20% of what was needed, well.....let's just say that was a revelation as uncomfortable as it was indisputable.

No amount of tact will allow a staffer to stay employed long if they insist on pointing out such difficult truths, especially when the congenial consulting engineer brushes the insight aside by noting — with not an ounce of irony — that, "We can't possibly know what will happen two or three decades from now."

This past weekend, Minnesota's newspaper of record — the Star Tribune — ran an article entitled, "As maintenance costs rise, homeowners ask cities to take over private streets." We can already see where this is going, can't we? From the article:

> *For residents, private streets offer seclusion and a lower upfront price tag. For developers, they're an opportunity to build without municipal costs and design constraints. But homeowners in Rosemount and elsewhere, faced with road maintenance costs that will only rise as streets age, are asking local officials to make their streets public.*
>
> *"It's going to be a huge cost to rebuild in the future, 20 years down the road," Rehman said. "It doesn't make sense to have homeowners pick up that kind of cost."*[xxx]

It's a very strange place that we've come to in America where that last sentence can be spoken, let alone printed. Almost all private roads are, by definition, closed systems; loops or dead end cul-de-sacs. Their only reason for existing is to serve the property owners along them. They have no other function.

If it "doesn't make sense" for the people that live along a dead end road to pick up the cost of maintaining it, what *does* make sense? In the Ponzi scheme that is the financing of America's suburbs, local government, the magical entity that — while it is made up of a collection of neighborhoods of people — is somehow expected to provide more services and amenities than those people are willing to pay for. From the article:

> *The private model works as long as homeowners associations have the spending power and wherewithal to keep up with maintenance. But for those that haven't planned well or simply can't afford it, future fixes loom large.*
>
> *"It's not surprising that some of them might have said, 'Well, we might have made this deal originally, but we'd rather have the government take care of these things,'"* Nelson said.[xxxi]

The fascinating thing about these transactions — private roads becoming public — is that they make no financial sense for the other property owners in the city. Zero. The homeowners with the private road are already paying taxes to the local government. Those taxes don't go up at all when the city takes over their road; the city gets zero additional revenue. Yet now the city must take money from everyone else to subsidize the costs of these once-private roads. Why do cities regularly do this?

Well, if you believe in the wealth enhancing notion of a "free road" or if you believe that there is an overriding public interest in the city owning every possible square feet of asphalt (streets are assets,[xxxii] after all), then it might. And, in the narrow vision of the bureaucratic silo where codes and hierarchy are paramount concerns, all we need to make this good is to have the private road brought up to the divine standards of the city. Again, from the article:

> *"We heard a lot of people say, 'We pay taxes just like everyone else, yet we have to maintain our own streets,'" said City Engineer Larry Poppler. "That was kind of the cry from a number of neighborhoods."*
>
> *In response, the city created a policy in 2009 that requires homeowners to go through a multi-step process, including obtaining the consent of all their neighbors, before their street can be made public. A big part of that process is bringing the street up to municipal standards, so the city isn't saddled with a rundown street. But for homeowners, those fixes can cost thousands of dollars.*[xxxiii]

It's astounding how we're so trained to think in one life cycle, to never ponder the long term maintenance costs. If property owners can't afford to pay for a smaller, less engineered road how does widening, straightening, flattening and making it more intensely engineered suddenly make it affordable?

Back in 2012, I wrote a piece called *Assessing our Future*[xxxiv] about the process local governments use to illegally extract money from property owners through the assessment process. I provided this after-the-fact analysis for cities now struggling to pay for roads they never should have taken over:

> *It is public infrastructure, taken over by the city for*

maintenance through a public process, and it is now the city's to maintain at full cost of that maintenance, minus any increase in property value the project might create. If the city did not think this infrastructure served a public purpose, it should not have taken it over and assumed the maintenance liability.

Expect to see this kind of nonsense as we watch more and more of America's suburbs and exurbs enter the terminal Desperation Phase of the Growth Ponzi Scheme. We Americans have an incredible ability to delude ourselves; the absurd notion that local governments (a collection of us) can step in where property owners can no longer afford their own private roads is just another variation on that theme. As Strong Towns advocates, we can't prevent mass delusion, but we *can* work to establish an alternative model for achieving prosperity so there is a viable option to hysteria (and all it's handmaidens) when the Illusion of Wealth vanishes. We need to start building strong towns.

#NoNewRoads

Section II: Slow the Cars

If you need a sign to tell people to slow down, you designed the street wrong.

#slowthecars

7. SLOW THE CARS
by Charles Marohn

(January 1, 2015) For those of you that drive, I'd like you to start taking note of something. I'd like you to mentally document the way that pedestrians act at crosswalks. When you approach a crosswalk and someone is trying to walk across the street, look at how they respond to your presence.

If they are like most people, they will do something to pick up their pace and clear the intersection more quickly. They'll walk faster. They might even run. I've even seen people retreat back to the side of the road then wave me – the driver – through.

Now think of approaching that same intersection except, instead of a pedestrian crossing, there is someone in another car. What does that other driver do? Do they pick up their pace to clear the intersection for you? Do they retreat whence they came and wave you through? Of course not.

Why the difference?

The obvious answer would be the asymmetry of danger

between the pedestrian and the automobile driver, the former being far more vulnerable. That might be the case in some instances, but you can observe people rushing across the street even when the car is fully stopped, the driver has made eye contact and there is no real risk.

I think a more pernicious reason for this behavior is that many – perhaps most – Americans today have accepted the notion that streets are for cars. Period. Anyone not in a car might be allowed in this space as a courtesy, but the paved street is – first and foremost – the dominion of cars.

Last week someone sent me a video on pedestrian safety from the Des Moines police department.[xxxv] While very well-intentioned, I found the premise to be incredibly disturbing. First, they state that there is confusion over who has the right-of-way at "intersections and at crosswalks." Okay, but then they add this:

"The biggest problem drivers face is being able to understand all the different types of pedestrian signs."

Say what?

Now, to cut the police a little slack, their role in this crazy system is to maintain order. There is nothing more orderly than a bunch of signs and a plethora of laws telling us where each type is to be deployed and how everyone is legally required to act at said deployment. I'm not shocked that the Des Moines police department might view this as a regulatory problem.

Still....drivers are having trouble understanding the signs? So, if every driver clearly saw and understood the signs but pedestrians were still getting mowed down – or, more likely, people were simply choosing not to walk because they did not feel safe or comfortable doing so – that would be okay? It would be orderly, but that is clearly not the optimum outcome.

One of my twin hometowns – Baxter, the fully suburban one – took this thinking to the next illogical step in a recent project they completed. Along their expanded stroad are not only signs for a pedestrian crossing, just in case one encounters that sub-variant species rarely found in suburbia, *Homo sapien carless*, but they actually each have a sign telling you there is a sign coming up. Very orderly. Very dumb.

This is all to be expected, however, for a centralized system like ours. What drives the mission and focus of all these local street departments is the funding, and the biggest source of that is often the federal government. We adopt their standards because we're using their funding.

For instance, the bible for placing signage is a book known as the Manual on Uniform Traffic Control Devices (MUTCD). The Federal Highway Administration version of the MUTCD – think of it as Patient Zero – defines a street as "see Highway".[xxxvi] It then defines "Highway" as:

> *Highway—a general term for denoting a public way for purposes of vehicular travel, including the entire area within the right-of-way.*

The mentality of our entire system – and subsequently everything we communicate to driver and pedestrian alike – is that the street is the sole dominion of the automobile. Everything and everyone else is an interloper to be tolerated, at best. Is it any wonder people don't feel safe outside of a car?

And if you think that is too harsh, consider this paradox: When we design for fast-moving traffic, we go to great lengths to remove obstacles from the clear zone; things like a tree or a wall. Anything we have to place in this clear zone we then require to be "breakaway" so that it gives way when a car collides with it. I've even seen state DOTs demand that retailers remove sandwich board signs on the sidewalk, not because it was distracting but because the signs could damage a vehicle if the vehicle went off the stroad and hit them.

We go through all this trouble to make things safe for vehicles and their drivers, but then we allow – and even design for – people to be in this space. We put sidewalks right on the edge of roadways that we post at 45 mph, a speed that we know will kill someone who is outside of a vehicle.

Perhaps traffic engineers are not offended by this. Pedestrians are technically "breakaway" as well and thus meet their design requirements.

So we tolerate pedestrians, essentially at their own risk. If we wanted to build streets to not simple tolerate pedestrians but to actually accommodate people – who, by the way, are the main indicator species of a financially productive place – what would we do differently?

Someone sent me one of those articles that details the history of automobile/pedestrian interaction.[xxxvii] This one was in Collector's Weekly and was a great read. The most amazing part – and the answer to making streets that are financially productive once more – is the different attitude towards pedestrians. From the article:

> *[Historically] roads were seen as a public space, which all citizens had an equal right to, even children at play. "Common law tended to pin responsibility on the person operating the heavier or more dangerous vehicle," says [Peter] Norton, "so there was a bias in favor of the pedestrian." Since people on foot ruled the road, collisions weren't a major issue: Streetcars and horse-drawn carriages yielded right of way to pedestrians and slowed to a human pace. The fastest traffic went around 10 to 12 miles per hour, and few vehicles even had the capacity to reach higher speeds.*[xxxviii]

As the article went on, it detailed things such as "silent policeman" and "traffic turtles" that essentially thwarted the speed ambitions of drivers so as to keep the public realm safe for everyone. The expectations were different:

> *If a kid is hit in a street in 2014, I think our first reaction would be to ask, 'What parent is so neglectful that they let their child play in the street?,' says Norton.*
>
> *In 1914, it was pretty much the opposite. It was more*

> like, 'What evil bastard would drive their speeding car where a kid might be playing?' That tells us how much our outlook on the public street has changed—blaming the driver was really automatic then. It didn't help if they said something like, 'The kid darted out into the street!,' because the answer would've been, 'That's what kids do. By choosing to operate this dangerous machine, it's your job to watch out for others.' It would be like if you drove a motorcycle in a hallway today and hit somebody—you couldn't say, 'Oh, well, they just jumped out in front of me,' because the response would be that you shouldn't operate a motorcycle in a hallway."[xxxix]

The forgiving design principles that traffic engineers employ have replaced the "that's what kids do" burden on the driver with a "that's what drivers do" burden on all of society. If we want to make our cities prosperous again, we have to return that burden to the driver. Not just at intersections. Not just where there are properly specified signs. It is their burden, their responsibility, everywhere, all the time. Period.

Now here's the catch: We need to design our streets to reflect that reality. We need to design our streets so that drivers feel unsafe driving at speeds that are unsafe. That's an entirely different America than the one we live in now, but one that's actually less expensive to build and more financially successful once completed.

#SlowtheCars

8. A STATISTICALLY INEVITABLE OUTCOME
by Charles Marohn

(February 16, 2015) The light turned signaling it was safe to walk. A four-year-old boy took his mother's hand. Together they stepped out into the crosswalk on their way to a pre-kindergarten class at the Philip Schuyler Achievement Academy in Albany, NY. A garbage truck came around the corner and they were run down. The boy was killed, the mother's life horribly changed forever.

This particular incident happened in February of 2015,[xl] but something like it will happen somewhere else today. This kind of tragedy happens again and again, day after day, because our streets are not safe. Imagine this scene from the article replayed thousands of times each year here in America:

> *Passerby Gerron Zeigler saw the aftermath of the crash and recalled a woman screaming, "They took my son! They took my son!" after the child was put in an ambulance.*[xli]

The anguish of this family is too painful to think about.

I don't know what happened in this particular case, but from reading the article I can tell that we're taking in all the wrong lessons. The first — labeling this an "accident" — comes from a woman identified as an "educator and administrator" ostensibly from the school this family was trying to reach. Here is her statement:

> *As an educator and administrator, Vanden Wyngaard admitted that she never stops worrying about student safety and their abilities to get home, but she doesn't think this should be a deterrent to students walking to school. Instead, she said, Thursday was a tragic reminder that accidents happen.*[xlii]

Let's be clear: This isn't an accident. According to Google, an accident is defined as, "an event that happens by chance without an apparent cause."[xliii] While there is certainly an element of chance here — just as with Russian Roulette — there is obviously an underlying, preventable cause.

This intersection is really dangerous for people outside of a vehicle. Serious injury is statistically inevitable. The design of this space induces high vehicle speeds in a complex environment not conducive to high speeds. There is only superficial protection for pedestrians and bikers. Indeed, the reporter on the scene was able to speak to someone who had seen a similar incident in the recent past:

> *Linda McClean, who has worked the morning shift at the Subway sandwich shop across Central Avenue from the crash for four years, said the intersection with Quail Street as seen through the store's wall of windows is*

busy with traffic and can be dangerous to pedestrians. She saw a person get hit in the same intersection last summer.[xliv]

Let's look at the ways in which this design is deadly for people outside of a vehicle.

THE APPROACH

Image from Google Maps[xlv]

Here's the approach to the intersection. Note the sedan in the right lane. It's about six feet wide. Discounting the unused parking lane, based on the sedan we can say that there is at least twelve feet of width in that right lane. This is a highway dimension being incorrectly applied to this street by the design engineers. Their false belief is that a wide lane is safer because it provides recovery area for the driver. It might serve that function on a highway, but on a city street it gives the driver a false sense of a safety margin and, in doing so, encourages speeds beyond what is safe in such an environment.

That sense of a safety margin is enhanced by the lack of any vertical element such as street trees or lighting. (There are street trees further down the street, but not here.) In this particular instance, the long, vacant wall presented by

Subway signals no activity (i.e. nothing to be concerned with) to the driver. All the messages presented to the driver here say: wide open stretch, no inherent danger. That's by design.

Also note that there's nobody parked here, which is also by design. While you are allowed to park here, the parking appears to be metered. You have to pay. Now I'm not against paid parking, but the supply/demand necessities to fill these spots is obviously not present.

A further look at Google Maps shows that surface parking in the area is abundant. It's not clear whether or not the off-street parking is metered, but from Google maps, it doesn't appear to be in heavy use. This kind of thing happens all the time. The city demands parking, the neighborhood demands parking and the businesses want parking, so off-street parking is provided. In addition to facilitating (sometimes even requiring) this really destructive practice, the city also lacks the sophistication to adjust the pricing of on-street parking to make it competitive. The spots then go unfilled and the protective barrier of parked cars is absent.

In theory, that extra space not being used by a parked car provides a greater safety margin for the driver. The driver now has an extra nine feet to play with as a recovery area. By the standard logic of the engineering profession, this is safer for everyone. In practice, the result is higher automobile speeds in a complex, urban environment.

THE INTERSECTION

So now we have fast-moving vehicles approaching the intersection just a couple blocks from a school where we anticipate that people — especially small children —and cyclists may be present. The street should have been designed to slow cars and trucks down before they reached the intersection, but the industry's standard approach worries primarily about the free flow of traffic. This value system is also apparent within the intersection.

Arrow indicates excessive curb radius. Image from Google Maps[xlvi]

The picture above shows the street corner where the boy and his mom were standing waiting to cross. Note the curve of the curb. This is called the curb radius. The larger the radius, the more gradual the curve and the easier it is for a vehicle to take the corner without slowing down. In a paradigm where traffic flow is the primary concern and the safety of drivers is the secondary concern (with the safety of those outside a vehicle being a far distant concern by comparison), the standard industry practice is to have as large of a radius as possible.

I drew in the lines on the pavement to mark the area that exists solely to allow drivers to move their vehicle through the intersection more quickly. Note that on both streets this is the parking area so it is not part of the oncoming traffic lanes, yet it is left open for turning traffic to occupy. In a properly designed intersection — where the safety of people outside of their vehicles was a primary concern — this area would be devoted to people. It would be a bike/ped safety zone, not an auto acceleration zone.

For pedestrians and cyclists, intersections are really dangerous places. Slowing cars heading into the intersection, then keeping auto movements slow and deliberate within an intersection, are key safety strategies. In our segregated environment — one where we expect everyone to stay in their place and we handle overlaps by giving priority with a traffic signal — there are two important things that need to happen.

First, we need to limit the amount of time and space in which pedestrians and cyclists are exposed to cross traffic. Second, when pedestrians enter an intersection, they need to be given exclusive use of it. In other words, vehicles need to have all red lights. We cannot ethically expect people to dodge vehicles; the mismatch between a four-year-old and a garbage truck is too great.

Image from Google Maps[xlvii]

The image above shows the crossing (left) where the accident took place. On the right are two people attempting to cross. Note the huge width they need to traverse where they are completely exposed. I estimate it is 70 feet. These two people look relatively young and healthy, yet they've only made it halfway across when the pedestrian signal is telling them they are running out of time.

The car — which has the same inducements as the garbage truck to enter the intersection at high speeds — is pressing in on the vulnerable people. In some places such activity may be illegal, but it should not be unexpected given the design.

The driver here is taking advantage of the wide open intersection to cut the corner (the same way the garbage truck did).

MORE ENFORCEMENT?

I'm sympathetic to people who suggest that more enforcement is needed. I'm sympathetic, but I don't agree. I also don't agree that this is a matter of driver education or awareness. While it seems barbaric to have a driver speeding in a garbage truck take the life of an innocent child standing in a crosswalk, how much can we really blame the driver? Every signal this design gives is that it is safe to drive fast. In fact, if the speed limit here is 30 mph, the driver may not have even been breaking any laws. He had a green light, after all. I'm sure it all looked and felt safe.

Time and time again, driving through this intersection in the exact same way, the result is no harm to anyone. That's why we're comfortable calling this tragedy an accident. It seems like a random event. Only it's not.

This and the thousands of similar tragedies that happen every year on America's streets are the statistically inevitable outcome of designing for fast-moving traffic within a complex urban environment. This is what will always happen when we mash together simple and powerful with random and vulnerable. Our street designs do not account for the randomness of humanity. To be safe, they must.

It is no longer acceptable to design our urban streets to forgive the mistakes of drivers. Our designs must forgive the mistakes of the most vulnerable: those outside of a vehicle.

"They took my son! They took my son!"

#SlowtheCars

It's not a complete street unless it is completely safe.
#slowthecars

photo credit: Stephen Lee Davis / Transportation for America

9. THE FIGHT FOR PEDESTRIAN SAFETY
by Nathaniel Hood

(October 14, 2015) Getting even modest pedestrian improvements can be an uphill battle. We have a design bias that is inherently unfriendly to pedestrians and bicycles. While we've made great strides in the last decade, it's still a constant and frustrating battle.

Take a recent incident in Minneapolis as an example; a simple concrete median that protects pedestrians and bicycles is about to be removed. It comes after a dozen community meetings, a lengthy engagement process, broad-based community support, and the backing of local city council members.

Why is it being removed? Because a guy in Public Works doesn't like it. Apparently cars keep hitting it. *And therefore, it must be removed?* This may seem like a small deal, but it's not. It's an example of the uphill battle that bike and pedestrians advocates are fighting.

The system - as it is currently structured - is designed at every corner to favor the automobile.

It's so omnipresent that we often forget it exists. I was walking back from the St. Paul Farmer's Market in walkable Lowertown this last weekend and I was stopped in my tracks at the corner of 6th St & Sibley as a car whizzed by.

This is a great neighborhood that almost any urbanist would love. It's mixed-use, dense, has wide sidewalks, on-street parking, outdoor cafe seating, good public spaces, and plenty of eyes on the street. Yet, despite all these gains, there are still plenty of anti-urban transportation hold-outs present in the design. Here are three.

PROBLEM 1: THE CORNER

This radius of this corner was designed not to improve the safety of pedestrians, but to help cars make a right turn without having to slow down. This is a classic example of highway design being imposed on our downtowns. The goal of a city street should not be to maximize traffic flow.

When a street has a wider curve, vehicles can move around it much faster. When coupled with one-way streets, this can be even more dangerous. Simply reducing the corner radius can have a huge impact. This is a very simple, cost-effective way to improve walkability and pedestrian safety.

PROBLEM 2: ONE-WAY STREETS

The verdict is out, and it's been out for a long time. Yet, multi-lane, one-way couplings still exist in most of our downtowns.

I don't like writing about this because it's so obvious. One-way streets are bad for everyone except speeding cars.[xlviii] The struggle is that most of our American downtowns are held hostage by a commuter culture. Politicians and traffic engineers are hesitant to disrupt that culture. It's a shame, because they should.

Eric Jaffe at CityLab lists the most obvious reasons:

- ***Livability***: *vehicles stop less on one-way streets, which is hard for bikers and pedestrians.*
- ***Navigation***: *one-way street networks are confusing for drivers, which leads to more vehicle-miles traveled; they also make it tough for bus riders to locate stops for a return trip.*
- ***Safety***: *speeds tend to be higher on one-way streets, and some studies suggest drivers pay less attention*

to them because there's no conflicting traffic flow.
- **Economics**: local businesses believe that two-way streets increase visibility.[xlix]

One-way streets are a transportation relic that need to be expelled in almost all cases. We need to value livability, navigation, safety, and economics above the desire to travel fast in an automobile.

PROBLEM 3: UNNECESSARY TURN LANES

Every turn lane imposed on the urban environment where it is not needed does three things:

- **Increases crossing distance:** Pedestrians are in the intersection — where they're most likely to be injured — for an additional 10 to 13 feet.
- **Reduces size of sidewalk:** Turn lanes create less space for people to walk or for a business to have outdoor seating or displays.
- **Eliminates on-street parking:** Turn lanes remove an important safety buffer, and each on-street parking space is one that doesn't need to be expensively built off-street.

The dynamic needs to shift, and it needs to shift quickly.

The intersection I'm describing in St. Paul is actually *okay* for walkability, particularly when compared to what most American intersections looks like. This is a problem. We shouldn't have a system where these auto-biases are built so ubiquitously. We shouldn't have a system where — after lots of effort and community support — an infrastructure improvement can be overruled because a person at Public Works doesn't like it.

The American transportation system is designed at every corner to favor the automobile. It's a mindset that needs to change.

#SlowtheCars

10. GROSS NEGLIGENCE

by Charles Marohn

The next three pieces were the most important work we did in 2015. At least, it's the work I'm most proud of. Our #SlowtheCars campaign combines everything we are most passionate about: improved design of our places, embracing complexity, giving our cities back to people and a realization that a good financial strategy is also humane.

Each and every day, I see way too many people – the forgotten and overlooked in our community – struggling on foot to navigate the nasty streets we have built. When it snows, as it does often here in Minnesota, the ditches and alleys that are the safer routes become impassable. When the streets are most slippery and dangerous, the walkers and wheelchairs line them, just feet away from drivers navigating at fatal speeds.

What are we doing? Is this the world we want to live in?

The sad reality of it for me is that I didn't start off with concern for the people on the side of the road. I subconsciously dismissed them like most everyone else, an easy thing to do at 45 mph. For me it was the realization that this approach was bankrupting us – literally forcing cities into steep decline – that got me looking for answers.

And I found them. They were there on the side of the road. There they are, showing us what needs to be done to make our places better, stronger and more successful. We don't need megaprojects, massive highway expansions and debt. All we have to do is observe where people struggle and then take the next smallest step to address those struggles.

Making our cities easier to walk and bike is the lowest risk, highest returning investment we can make. It's also the most humane.

In 2014, I wrote in a piece called, "Just another pedestrian killed" about how the cruel design of a street in Springfield, Massachusetts – a design that facilitated auto traffic at convenient speeds but attempted to force, through the use of fences and other obstacles, people to walk 1,000+ feet out of their way just to cross the street – resulted in the death of a beautiful little girl.[l] I'm heartened to say that the people of Springfield still care; they are not letting this one go. They are still out there demanding change.[li]

Let's do that in every city. Let's not allow this continue any longer.

11. DODGING BULLETS
by Charles Marohn

(June 8, 2015) At basic training for the U.S Army, we did an exercise late one night where my fellow trainees and I were prompted to crawl about a hundred yards through a course containing barbed wire, trenches and other obstacles. We did this while machine gun fire blasted over our heads. I remember looking up and seeing the tracer rounds fly from a tower to a target back behind the course. The bullets were well over our heads — I am sure I could have stood up and they still would have been well above me — but it was disconcerting nonetheless. While it was very unlikely that I was going to be killed by a stray bullet, it was far more likely that I would be killed by one than my friends back home who weren't crawling beneath M-60 fire.

Imagine my drill sergeant set up an M-60 nest in the middle of the street, pointed it at a nice big target in the middle of the street a couple blocks away, then began firing from one to the other. He'd hit the target every time — he's a pro — and so there would be little to no risk of getting hit.

Now here's the question: Would you walk along the street?

Probably not. I wouldn't. In fact. I wouldn't let my kids go within six blocks of it if I knew this were going on. Is that irrational, especially since this is an expert marksman we're talking about? Statistically speaking, perhaps it is, but when a small mistake means the difference between life and death, why risk it? What is the upside that justifies the risk?

At the end of last month there was a terrible incident where a car left the roadway killing a child and injuring another who were walking through a park. Here's an excerpt from the news report:

> *A child is dead and another is in critical condition after a car struck them in Delaware Park.*
>
> *The vehicle left the road while traveling westbound on Route 198 - the Scajaquada Expressway - just past Parkside Avenue around 11:30 a.m. It struck a three year old boy who was taken to Sisters Hospital, where he was pronounced dead at 12:15 p.m. His five year old sister is in critical condition at Women & Children's Hospital.*
>
> *The two were out walking with their mother in the park, and one or both may have been seated in a stroller.*[lii]

Sadly, the unique thing about this incident is not the death of a child — children get run down and killed by vehicles all the time — the unique thing is the reaction to this specific tragedy.

In the following days, New York Governor Andrew Cuomo ordered the speed on Highway 198, which runs right through

Delaware Park and bisects a number of community amenities and neighborhoods, to be reduced to 30 mph. His directive included the following:

> *While law enforcement agencies are still investigating the circumstances surrounding this terrible crash, it is clear that immediate action needs to be taken to improve safety for motorists and pedestrians on the portion of the Scajaquada Expressway that passes through Delaware Park.*
>
> *For this reason, I direct you to immediately lower the speed limit on this section of the roadway to 30 mph, install speed messaging boards, and construct park-appropriate guard rails to protect pedestrians.*
>
> *These actions are to be taken as the Department of Transportation continues to investigate long-term solutions to prevent further tragedies on this part of the Expressway.*
>
> *This administration will continue to take every available action we can through engineering, education and enforcement to avoid crashes like this in the future.*[liii]

This might seem logical to many of you, but I want to direct your attention to a nuance demonstrating confusion over the tradeoffs we make each day when designing our transportation systems.

The governor has directed the DOT to (1) lower the speed limit and install the signs that indicate this, and (2) build guard rails. In the language we use at Strong Towns, Cuomo is saying, (1) make Highway 198 more like a street and, (2) make Highway 198 more like a road. In other words, stop firing bullets, but also put up protective barriers.

The question we should be asking here is this: Is Highway 198 a road or a street? Is it a connection between two productive places OR is it a platform for creating wealth?

If it's a road, which it seems like to me, then lowering the speed limit is the wrong thing to do. With the way this highway is engineered for high speeds, an artificially low speed limit will create a dangerous situation. If this is going to be designated a 30 mph stretch (still too fast to be compatible with people outside of their cars), then the roadway needs to be redesigned so that the typical driver only feels comfortable when driving at safe, neighborhood speeds. Lowering the speed limit might be good politics — it is an action that can be taken immediately to give the appearance of doing something — but it's not good policy, even as an interim step. Sending mixed signals to driver – design says to drive fast and the law says to drive slow – is dangerous to everyone.

How about the guard rails? Again, if we're building a road where the goal is moving cars quickly, then the guardrails are a good interim step, but long term we will need something more robust to keep people and traffic safely separated. I note that the governor called for "park-appropriate" guard rails, which I take to mean guard rails that won't harm the view of the park as seen from the driver's seat. If that's the case, then we're confusing the purpose of a park here just as badly as we're confusing the purpose of a highway.

Urban parks are not aesthetic amenities for passing motorists. There's no return on that investment. Urban parks are meant to provide value — improve the quality of life — to people living within walking, biking or transit distance of the park. If we're doing it right, that value should be reflected in the value of the tax base, the real creation of wealth.

All of this confusion goes back, of course, to the original bad decision to run a highway through the middle of a neighborhood. You have a park, a college, the river and lots of housing. These investments should not have been so casually disregarded, but they were.

If Buffalo today were to eliminate Highway 198 — turn it into a true parkway with 20 mph neighborhood design speeds — I would applaud. I'm guessing that many in the neighborhood would as well. After a transition, there would be many opportunities for growing the tax base and leveraging the parking to grow the community's wealth. Unfortunately, for a whole bunch of reasons, I doubt this will happen.

If it doesn't, that leaves Buffalo with only two other viable options: Build your barriers high and thick to protect people from stray cars OR accept a certain level of tragic, random death and injury as a byproduct of the stroad you have built. Both of these are expensive, unproductive and just plain sad uses of public resources.

If bullets were being expertly fired by a marksman at a target along Highway 198, New Yorkers would go berserk, even though the chance of accidental death would be minimal. I would not blame them for this reaction, but I'm completely baffled as to why we accept much greater risk when it's from a driver and their automobile. I also don't know why we continue to accept incoherent, half-measures as a response.

Put in a real barrier to make it a road or slow the cars to make it a street. The continued street/road hybrid approach of this and countless other stroads is only going to lead to more needless tragedy, with the side effect of our cities going bankrupt in the process.

#SlowtheCars

12. THE BOLLARD DEFENSE
by Charles Marohn

(June 9, 2015) In writing about the tragedy in Buffalo where a three year old was killed, and his five year old sister injured, when they were struck by a vehicle that had jumped the from the stroad, my objective was to point out how the governor's response — an action I'm quite sure is a popular one — doubles down on the stroad mentality: lower speeds (as a street) and erect guard rails (as a road). We're stuck in a destructive mindset and our cities won't get systematically better until we grow out of it.

The Buffalo case isn't the most bizarre response I've seen, however. I've been sitting on the one I'm going to share here for a while — there are just so many — but now is a good time to put it out there. I apologize in advance because this one is even more sickening than the last.

Out of Orlando; here's the lead from the article:

> *Florida Highway Patrol troopers said Lily Quintus, 4, of Orlando died following a car crash at a day care in Orange County Wednesday afternoon.*

A small memorial for Quintus was set up at the KinderCare center by Wednesday night.

Robert Corchado, 28, was named a suspect in connection with the crash that injured 15 at the day care on Goldenrod Road near University Boulevard. He may be trying to leave Orlando, authorities said.

Florida Highway Patrol troopers said they believe Corchado, the driver of a silver Dodge Durango, rear-ended a Toyota Solara, which crashed into the building.

The car wound up inside the front room and was removed around 6:45 p.m. The driver of the Toyota wasn't injured.

Eight children were taken to Arnold Palmer Hospital.[liv]

Please note that I'm not sharing this one because it involves children — if my goal was to shock you with tragic child death stories, I could do that multiple times a week because that's how many kids are killed on our stroads — I'm sharing it because of the policy response.

Here's the view of the daycare (on the right) from the stroad:

Image from Google Maps[iv]

A classic Florida stroad; part street, part road, it combines fast moving cars with turning traffic directly adjacent to pedestrians. This is the most dangerous, costly and financially unproductive investment a city can make.

Car leaves the stroad, smashes into another car which smashes into a daycare killing one child and injuring many others.

What do the adults here do to keep their kids safe? Do they slow the traffic speed? Do they address the incompatibility of having highway speed vehicles on a nasty, complex stroad just feet from the doorway to the facility? Do they look at the sidewalks built directly adjacent to vehicles traveling at highway speeds and think it strange, even barbaric, that we would place anyone — let alone young children — in such a dangerous environment?

No. A year later, the answer here is — as it always is — more armor and more padding. From the Orlando Sentinel:

> Where once there was only a hedge, now five heavy planters and six concrete spheres stand guard in front of the building, presenting a barrier designed to protect

> *those inside should another vehicle come careening toward it.*
>
> *And plans are underway that could make such barriers standard at day-care centers around Orange County.*[lvi]

That's right. We now have our children ensconced behind a barrier of protective concrete as if they were in the US Green Zone in Iraq. Is this really how we intend to raise the next generation?

Our responses never question the contradictions of a stroad but instead take fast-moving cars in a complex environment as the absolute, unquestioned way things must be. Nonetheless, the decision to armor the daycare was not made without deliberation or an understanding of the extent of the problem. Again from the Orlando Sentinel article:

> *In the days after that incident, Mayor Teresa Jacobs directed county staff from various departments to look at how much of a public-safety threat vehicle crashes pose to "vulnerable" populations such as children and seniors.*
>
> *The KinderCare crash was the result of a mix of factors — an initial crash involving two vehicles, followed by one driver failing to brake and hitting the day care center.*
>
> *"The numbers are pretty stark," [Fire Chief Otto Drozd] said. "What we found is nationally there's 60 a day, causing almost 4,000 injuries and 500 deaths a year."*
>
> *Locally, the team found 73 incidents in which vehicles hit buildings in unincorporated Orange County over a*

> *24-month span, resulting in 37 people requiring a trip to the hospital.*
>
> *They found an additional 1,800 "road departures" — instances of vehicles losing control and leaving the roadway, but not striking buildings — over a 15-month span.*[lvii]

Understand what you're reading: five hundred deaths per year from cars leaving the road and striking a building and our response is more concrete barriers? The article continues:

> *The main methods to safeguard structures against vehicle impacts would be walls, planters, purpose-designed outdoor furniture or bollards, which are posts or spheres designed as traffic impediments.*
>
> *Most bollards are roughly waist-high, and can be made of concrete, steel, cast iron or even recycled plastic. The spherical bollards are a common sight outside of stores such as Target.*
>
> *Drozd said bollards generally cost about $450 apiece. He estimates it would cost about half a million dollars to protect all the vulnerable day-care facilities in unincorporated Orange County.*
>
> *Future day care centers would be expected to incorporate the safety features before opening. But funding for existing facilities to make the upgrades could come largely from government grants, Drozd said.*[lviii]

So let's raise everyone's taxes to build more stroads, so that we can then raise everyone's taxes more to provide grants to build concrete barriers to keep us safe from cars careening off our stroads. All so we can have a debt economy of crappy fast food, low wage jobs and national chain stores.

Aren't you sick of this?

#SlowtheCars

Thoughts on Building Strong Towns, Vol. II

A TRAGIC IRONY

Our wide streets allow us to quickly respond to collisions caused by our wide streets.

13. JUST AN ACCIDENT
by Charles Marohn

(June 9, 2015) I've got one more story of a terrible incident where an automobile struck children along our nation's stroads. This one will hopefully move us from what needs to be done (#SlowtheCars on our streets, de-stroad our roads) to who is responsible for leading the effort

And let me preview my answer for you: The engineering profession has a moral obligation to lead the effort to address this problem. They are the only ones who can do this effectively. Without them, it won't happen.

An all-too-familiar story out of Springfield, Oregon, from this past February:

> Police said 68-year-old Larry LaThorpe of Springfield was behind the wheel of a pickup truck when it went through the intersection of 54th and Main streets. The truck hit and killed 8-year-old John Alexander Day; 5-year-old Mckenzie Mae Hudson; and 4-year-old Tyler

James Hudson.Medics took their mother, Cortney Jean Hudson, 26, of Springfield, to the hospital with serious injuries.She was listed in fair condition Tuesday at a local hospital.[lix]

This tragedy occurred at the intersection of 54th Street and Main Street, one of this country's ubiquitous stroad environments. Here's what the intersection looks like. I'm sure your community has lots of these.

Image from Google Maps[lx]

This being the third time through a tragic story like this, the response should now be anticipated by the reader. People are horrified at the tragic loss of innocent life. Temporary memorials are erected. Community dialog begins. Consensus emerges around a set of responses:

> *City officials and residents are proposing safety improvements after a driver struck and killed three children in a busy Springfield, Oregon, intersection last month. The City Council is discussing safety proposals at a meeting Monday night.*
>
> *Mayor Christine Lundberg told The Register-Guard*

> *newspaper she wants everything on the table. Ideas range from increased enforcement to more public safety announcements.*[lxi]

Public safety announcements, as if three dead kids — among scores of others killed around the country each year — isn't announcement enough. Understand that fourteen people have died on this particular Main Street in the past decade.[lxii] FOURTEEN! You'd think those deaths would be enough of a public service announcement.

Now to be fair, there were other proposals beyond enforcement and education that were put on the table. Although it was labeled "complicated," there was some mention of traffic calming:

> *They include reducing speeds on the corridor either by lowering speed limits or narrowing the travel lanes to give motorists a visual cue they need to slow down. Both would require ODOT approval.*
>
> *The speed limit is 40 mph along most of the corridor, but it increases to 45 at the eastern end.*[lxiii]

These are complicated, of course, because it would "require ODOT approval." Read: not going to happen.

Among the hundreds of similar tragedies I could highlight — the list is endless — I've picked this one because of an editorial column that came with it. The editorial board of the Oregonian weighed into this debate with "When a tragic accident is just a tragic accident,"[lxiv] a piece that acknowledged the tragedy while also acknowledging the fact that it is really, really difficult to condemn a person — lock them up — for something that was not related to how they were operating but merely a matter of chance; bad timing in a situation that any of us who drive could find ourselves in.

> *There are few words as inadequate as "accident" in describing a tragedy of this magnitude. It's hard not to feel outrage that LaThorpe isn't being held criminally accountable for a clear failure with such devastating consequences. How can there be no one to pay for the violent deaths these three kids suffered?*
>
> *But as wholly unsatisfying as it may be, "accident" is the only way to accurately describe what unfolded at that intersection on Feb. 22. Investigators found no evidence that LaThorpe was impaired, using a phone or speeding. And while the community may be searching for a way to ease its grief, prosecutors cannot look to heartbreak and anger as the building blocks of a case.*[lxv]

Even though I know that is going to anger some of you, I agree with the Oregonian. *But Chuck....if you're driving a big truck, you suffer the consequences of your actions. Those kids get no second chance. Throw the driver in jail and hide the key.*

While I understand this reaction, I don't find it helpful because it ignores the reality that someone can operate a vehicle as it's designed, following the rules of the environment it is designed for, doing so with all prudence and seriousness and they can *still* wind up killing someone.

Many times a driver is at fault and, if that's the case, convict them. But many times it is random chance, the statistically predictable outcome of millions of chance interactions between fast moving cars and complex environments that we have designed into our system.

I have an answer to this: eliminate stroads. We need to either convert our stroads into slow moving streets that are safe for everyone or make them high speeds roads that connect productive places with safe corridors that are free from turning traffic, pedestrians and other complex movements. It's either a street or a road and the design must reflect that.

So who is responsible for this? The Oregonian editorial points us in the right direction:

> *Lane County District Attorney Alex Gardner sought to provide some of that legal background in his press release announcing the decision not to charge LaThorpe. He quoted from a 2014 Oregon Court of Appeals decision in a case where a 17-year-old Curry County girl crashed into and killed a motorcyclist when she fell asleep at the wheel. In overturning her conviction, the judges said criminally negligent homicide requires proof "that the defendant should have been aware of a problem with the defendant's driving, such as swerving, inattention, or near collisions," before the crash.*
>
> *Another case, decided in 1978, established "that mere inadvertence, brief inattention, or error in judgment as to proper speed does not constitute gross negligence" unless there's a component of recklessness – such as drinking – or a "conscious indifference to the safety of others."*[lxvi]

Focus on that last part of that last sentence; a conscious indifference to the safety of others. In order to be found guilty of gross negligence, you must display a conscious indifference to the safety of others. Keep that in mind as you consider the stroads where the five child deaths I just highlighted took place.

Who is showing a conscious indifference to the safety of others? In other words, who is grossly negligent? Is it the driver who is following the speed limit, operating a vehicle well below the much higher design speed? Or is it whoever decided that 45+ mph traffic should be feet away from kids biking on the sidewalk, moms with strollers and children waiting to be picked up from daycare?

Is it the driver — a mere mortal suffering a predictable, perhaps even understandable moment of inattention or confusion while performing the monotony that we call driving — or is it the person who took 70 mph highway design standards and applied them to urban streets?

Is it the driver, whose path has been cleared of every foreseeable obstacle in a desperate effort to gain them seconds' worth of performance, or is it the person who apparently believes it is optimal to have no less than a quarter mile distance between each seven lane pedestrian crossing?

Who is the one showing conscious indifference to others? Who is grossly negligent?

It's not a person; it's a profession. The engineering profession — with a growing number of notable exceptions — employs a systematic approach to design, prioritizing the fast and efficient movement of automobiles over everything else, including safety. As a general rule, engineers show a conscious indifference to pedestrians and cyclists, misunderstanding their needs where they are not disregarded completely. This is the very definition of gross negligence.

This system can't be changed by engineers alone, but they are the only ones that can credibly lead the charge. A new mindset among my fellow engineers would be game-changing and is long overdue.

#SlowtheCars

14. GRANULARITY
by Andrew Price

(October 21, 2015) The word 'granular' is used to describe something that is made up of smaller elements, and 'granularity' is how small or large those elements are. If the elements are small, we call it 'fine-grained', and if the elements are large we call it 'coarse-grained'. It is a term we use in economics, computer science, geology, and likely many other fields. For example, in computer science, an algorithm is fine-grained if it is divided into many small steps, and coarse-grained if it is divided into few large steps.

When talking about cities, I use the term *granularity* to talk about how the ownership of a city is divided up, particularly in the size of the lots that city blocks are divided into. Here are some examples:

A block in Hoboken, NJ built out in the early 1900s with around 40 blocks per lot.

A new medium-rise apartment building in Hoboken taking up an entire block.

We can also talk about the granularity of an economy - an economy can be fine-grained if it is made up of many small businesses, coarse-grained if it is made up of few large businesses, and anywhere in between. Having a fine-grained economy made up of many small businesses is generally preferable over a coarse-grained economy made up of fewer businesses because the former implies a more resilient system (if one of the businesses fails, less is the effect on the overall economy) and more distributed wealth (the profit and ownership of the businesses are divided among many, rather than in the hands of a few).

Cities are the physical manifestation of the economy, and our built environment speaks volumes about our economy. It is easier to see this in smaller towns where the economic model is simplified — you can easily spot the difference between a small town dominated by a few large stores and a small town dominated by many smaller stores. There is often a correlation between the environment that we physically see and interact with, and the underlying economics that built it.

Although much of what I say here could be applied to suburban areas, I'm going to focus specifically on urban areas. Urban areas — our downtowns and our neighborhoods dominated by townhomes and apartments — the areas where we navigate on foot, are experienced in a fundamentally different way than auto-oriented, suburban areas.

The reason for this difference is that our sense of scale and place changes when we are walking (where there is only so far we can reasonably walk, and we are exposed to our environment) compared to when we are driving (where we can drive for miles with little effort, and we have little interest in how the realm outside of our car feels as we are confined in the comforts of our own cars).

Very few people talk about granularity, often ignoring it completely as we get excited over the next flashy megaproject.

Older urban areas in the United States are typically very

fine-grained. While newer urban areas in the United States typically are very coarse-grained.

BENEFITS OF FINE-GRAINED URBANISM

Fine-grained urbanism is preferable because it implies:

- **Diverse ownership.** Each individual lot typically has a different owner.
- **Lower cost of entry.** If we ignore the underlying price of land (small lots in general should be cheaper because you are buying less land), it takes less money to build a shop or a home on a small, narrow lot, than to build an entire apartment complex.
- **More destinations within walking distance.** An important part of good urbanism is fitting as much as possible within walking distance, so naturally fitting more in gives you a broader range of destinations to walk to.
- **Greater resistance to bad buildings.** Bad buildings make less of an impact when they are limited in size.

I am going to cover each of these points in detail.

Diverse ownership and lower cost of entry go hand in hand. It takes a lot of money to build a huge building. Ignoring land costs, this building could easily cost $30 million:

$30 million is a significant amount. It is far more than the typical middle-class person could afford. In contrast, any of these townhomes (also ignoring the land costs) could probably be built for less than $200,000. They are basic brick cubes with doors and windows:

It should really cost no more than a suburban house, minus the yard. Here is a slightly denser urban street, that should still be reasonably affordable to build:

Urban development should not be expensive by itself. I worry that the high cost of entry brought on by coarse-grained urbanism is leading to economic polarization — a situation where only those who already have money can invest and create more wealth, while everyone else is a mere consumer.

If we consider each building a destination, fine-grained urban areas are naturally more walkable because we have more destinations within walking distance than in coarse-grained urban areas. When your lots are only 20 feet wide, you are naturally going to have a destination (a building, an office, a shop, etc.) entrance every 20 feet along the street:

Fine-grained buildings along Washington Street, Hoboken.

In contrast, we have coarse-grained urbanism, where you have very few destinations, many taking up entire blocks:

If our destinations are only 20 feet wide rather than 200 feet wide, we can fit 10 times as many destinations along the same length of street.

There is also faux-granularity, which is when a large building is divided into many separate destinations at street level to get the impression of fine-grained urbanism:

This can solve the walkability issue with coarse-grained urbanism, but that is up to the discretion of the property owner. True fine-grained urbanism, however, forces this because each grain along the street is a destination; a building with no entrance is useless.

I do not think that all large buildings are bad. Some things, such as convention centers, sports stadiums, movie cinemas, and department stores naturally take up a lot of room and require large buildings. Like many things, coarse-grained development is acceptable when done in moderation, but when it becomes the default way of building, *that* is problematic. When we do need to build coarse-grained buildings though, it is important that we utilize faux-urbanism (which I'll discuss in a moment) to keep the area from becoming dull and barren.

Javits Center in Manhattan, a dead street.

Fine-grained development also limits the impact of bad buildings. A property owner that builds a dull or ugly building, allows their building to become run down, or abandons it, negatively affects the streetscape. However, we can minimize the overall impact to the streetscape if the ugly or derelict building is just one of many along the block.

FAUX-GRANULARITY

Faux-granularity is when we imitate the feel of a fine-grained place. There are places where fine-grained development is impractical, such as in high-rise central business districts where the economics of the place make really tall buildings feasible, and really tall buildings require large bases.

Large buildings are not bad when we use them in moderation. While it would be preferable to have a true fine-grained environment, we can do our best to imitate it.

Faux-granularity imitating a Main Street. Tanger Outlets in Atlantic City, NJ

We can imagine the worst-case scenario, which is a single building taking up an entire block, with a single entrance. When we remove the destinations along the street, we end up with a dead street - unsightly, unsafe, uninteresting. Even if you have nice architecture, the lack of the number of destinations to attract people really affects how interesting and alive the street feels.

We can easily imitate a fine-grained urban environment with faux-granularity. Some buildings, like convention centers, are naturally large scale and there is little we can do to avoid that. However, we should resist blank walls, which can lead to dead streets.

Dead streets are dangerous. They are the sorts of gray zones that Jane Jacobs talks about in *The Death and Life of Great American Cities*. Like oversized parks, dark alleys and underpasses, dead streets lack any sort of attraction to draw people. Not only are they unsightly, but the lack of people going about their businesses (what Jacobs calls "eyes on the street") often encourages crime.

Here is an example of a large building that uses faux-granularity to add a reasonable number of destinations that keep the street alive:

A very large building in Manhattan, but feels indistinguishable to walking past 8 separate buildings at street level. Image from Google Maps.[lxvii]

Faux-grained urbanism gives the feel of fine-grained urbanism, and for all practical purposes, functions the same as fine-grained urbanism as far as being interesting, attracting foot traffic, and being highly walkable. However, it does have some shortcomings that we should be aware of:

- It still consolidates a lot of the land into the hands of a single owner.
- It still has a high cost of entry to build.
- It is up to the discretion of the property owner if they decide to build faux-grained or if they build a blank wall.
- There is no resilience against a bad building. If the building is abandoned or has to be closed down, the entire block closes down. If the building is cheap and ugly, the entire block is cheap and ugly.

Faux-granularity is an example of treating the symptoms of disease (making coarse-grained urbanism work) rather than addressing the cause (which we could fix by building finer-grained buildings).

COARSE-GRAINED TENDENCY

There is a tendency for newer urban areas to be coarse-grained. Why?

A recent attempt to urbanize in Carmel, IN. Image from Google Maps.[lxviii]

I had a friend once tell me that the size of a development generally describes the size of the capital; someone with $1 billion in capital does not want to do 500, $2 million projects. This just raises more questions: Where are those with $2 million to spend? What about $200,000? Do a few at the top really own all of the wealth of the community? Is the lack of fine-grained urbanism a sign of corruption, that property development in your community is a game that only the already-wealthy can play?

I think a large part of the problem also lies in how we go about selling undeveloped land. A century ago, when a city found itself with land to sell off for development, it would plat the land and sell off the individual lots. Today, when cities find themselves with a parcel of land they want to sell, they will open up a bidding process for the whole thing.

This is also a cultural problem amongst New Urbanists. When you see an image of a New Urbanist plan, often it is some master planned, top-down, faux-grained vision, rather than something truly fine-grained.

Why aren't more planners dreaming and sketching varied, fine-grained blocks instead?

BUILDING FINE-GRAINED URBANISM

The most obvious solution for building fine-grained urbanism seems to be simply to plat out the land into smaller lots.

When a city finds itself in the possession of undeveloped land, it should take its best effort to divide it up and sell it in the smallest lot sizes as possible.

An alternative would be for a private developer to subdivide the land and sell off individual lots. This is similar to how suburban development works.

We could use a similar approach, both to build entirely new urban neighborhoods (similar to how the railroad companies of the 19th century would found new railroad towns by subdividing and selling off land in the middle of nowhere) and also at a much smaller scale to subdivide already existing blocks. For example, a developer could buy a large lot, build multiple buildings, then sell off each building individually for more than what they could from building and selling a single building.

You can tell that most likely a single developer built these due to the virtually identical architectural styles, but sold them off individually.

I saw this happening on a small scale when I was back in my home country of Australia. My aunt and uncle demolished their suburban home and subdivided their lot into three. They plan on building three townhomes, selling two and living in the third.

These are not the only ways we can build fine-grained urbanism, but they are a good place to start.

CONCLUSION

From an economic and an urbanist perspective, a fine-grained environment is a sign of a healthy city. Large buildings are not bad per se, and the best cities I have visited have a diverse mixture of large and small buildings. We should do our best to make our urban environment fine-grained, with development using as little land as possible. However, on the occasion when we do need to build large, we should do our best to make the result faux-grained.

The principle behind walkability and urbanism - and why I talk about granularity, non-places,[lxix] narrow streets,[lxx] and so on, is because walkability and urbanism are about fitting as much as you can within walking distance.

Treat land is if it is the most precious resource your city has. Never waste land or street space. Build real parks[lxxi] over greenspace.[lxxii] Create a place that is enjoyable and interesting, that encourages entrepreneurship, where you can mostly depend on your own two feet for daily errands. That is how you create a successful city.

All photographs by Andrew Price unless otherwise noted.

15. A STRONG TOWNS RESPONSE TO HOMELESSNESS
by Rachel Quednau

(January 28, 2015) In 2014, on any given night in January, more than 600,000 Americans were homeless.[lxxiii] That means they were sleeping in their car or under a bridge or in a temporary shelter in towns across America.

Most of the time when we see disabled veterans asking for change or single mothers waiting in line at food pantries, we turn away and ignore their presence in our towns. We even design our public spaces to try and prevent homeless people from being in them. But homelessness is an issue that we as Strong Citizens should care about. It impacts our cities. It impacts us. Put simply: Your town is not strong if some of your residents lack homes.

It is my belief that a Strong Town has available housing options for *all* of its residents, no matter their age, abilities or income. How can we get there in a practical and lasting manner?

First, a little history. One of the big reasons why homelessness has grown in the last fifty years is the loss of affordable housing, particularly Single Room Occupancy buildings or "SROs" which were historically a go-to option for low-income, single people. These apartments were built somewhat like dormitories, with bedrooms and very small or shared bathrooms and shared kitchens. They weren't perfect, but they provided dignity, independence and most importantly, housing for people who needed it. In the '70s and '80s, with the rise of the suburbs, McMansions and more single-family homes, many of these buildings with small units were knocked down under the guise of "urban renewal."

In order to reverse the tide of homelessness in this country, we will need to return to more modest housing options like the SROs of the past. Luckily, this country has seen a significant movement in that direction over the last several years. Here are some examples of what that looks like:

TENT CITIES

Tent cities have been a housing option for the homeless for many years. While they may have drawn attention during the Occupy Wall Street movement, they existed well before that. Naturally, when they are located in well-trafficked areas, tent cities often create a lot of conflict with the police, community leaders and neighbors — all of whom usually complain that they are dirty and dangerous. Those accusations are not always true.

For example, a few years ago in Champaign, IL, a tent city called Safe Haven developed (and was eventually demolished) on an empty lot in which homeless residents created a code of rules, kept one another safe, and even rented hygiene facilities. Tent cities are not the most permanent nor the most desirable option, but they provide an alternative to sleeping under a bridge or in a bus shelter.[lxxiv]

Think of it like guerrilla urbanism: We paint lines on the edge of streets that don't currently have sidewalks and a few years later, if enough people are walking in those areas, the hope is that the city government will come in and spend money on a real raised sidewalk. Similarly, if a tent city succeeds in a particular space, a developer could recognize its viability as a location for permanent affordable housing.

TINY HOMES

By now, most of you are probably familiar with the tiny home movement, and while it is primarily being spearheaded by the young, hip, DIY-crowd, it is slowly making inroads in homeless populations. In Madison, WI, for instance, community members designed a prototype tiny home village, complete with public spaces, gardens and artwork primarily to meet the needs of the homeless.[lxxv] In collaboration with architects, builders, and volunteers, homeless people are constructing their own tiny houses for very little money. It takes some finagling, particularly when faced with codes that exclude this sort of housing, but tiny homes builders are proving that it can be done in towns throughout the country.

MICROAPARTMENTS

Depending on the density of your city, microapartments might be the most realistic option for affordable housing. Microapartments are basically the modern SRO, except now they come with upscale amenities like tiny coffee makers that flip down from the wall, and little desks that can fold into drawers. They became particularly publicized after New

York City hosted a contest to design an affordable 200-350 square foot apartment a couple years ago.[lxxvi] It would be great to see more of these popping up in our towns, offering affordable housing for individuals and small families.

ACCESSORY DWELLING UNITS

Accessory Dwelling Units (ADUs) or "granny flats" are small homes that homeowners build onto their existing property—either as an attachment or as a detached unit. These can combat homelessness in a couple ways. First, they are usually very affordable to rent because they're small. Second, they are often used as a cheap or free housing option for elderly relatives of the homeowners, hence the term "granny flat." As horrible as it is to picture your grandfather homeless, seniors are one of the demographics that is quite vulnerable to homelessness because they are on fixed incomes and cannot always afford hikes in rent or property tax. Thus, by creating more accessory dwelling units, we open up options for seniors in our communities to live with people who can care for them.

Accessory dwelling units have been gaining traction over the last few years, although they often take a while to be approved by local governments.

In short, if we shift away from an insistence on large, suburban living quarters, we're much more likely to be able to meet the demand for housing for everyone. The creation of nontraditional, smaller and more affordable housing options is a vital step in ending homelessness and it's something that I hope to see more planners, politicians and developers tackling in the future.

But it is also something that everyday Strong Citizens can participate in. *You* can help build tiny homes and granny flats. *You* can advocate against the destruction of tent cities. *You* can attend the next meeting about a new apartment complex and encourage smaller, more affordable units.

If the goal is to move our cities in the direction of prosperity, we cannot accomplish it when a portion of our population is homeless. Government subsidies and temporary shelters are not a lasting solution to this issue, but affordable housing can be. Within the next decade, I hope to see more growth in affordable housing options like these, which have the potential to remove hundreds of thousands of people from situations of homelessness and enable our cities to be stronger and more resilient.

16. FIVE WAYS ENGINEERS DEFLECT CRITICISM
by Charles Marohn

(October 5, 2015) Transportation engineers can be intimidating. They are hard to oppose. When a member of the general public shows up at local meeting to express concern over a project — for example, their quiet local street being widened as if it were a highway — they more often than not find themselves verbally outgunned by the project engineer.

There are a handful of ways engineers deflect criticism. Chief among them is to resort to quoting industry standards. Having a huge budget and all the clout that comes with it doesn't hurt either. There are a number of well-worn threads I've heard engineers use time and again.

Earlier in this book (see Section II), we examined children being killed in automobile collisions, the conclusion of which was:

The engineering profession — with a growing number of

notable exceptions — employs a systematic approach to design prioritizing the fast and efficient movement of automobiles over everything else, including safety. As a general rule, engineers show a conscious indifference to pedestrians and cyclists, misunderstanding their needs where they are not disregarded completely. This is the very definition of gross negligence.

When we shared this on our website, some engineers on Reddit took exception to my assertion.[lxxvii] I've gone back over their critiques and identified the five most common lines I've heard engineers use to deflect criticism.

1. You Don't Have a Valid Opinion if You're Not a Licensed Engineer.

Getting an engineering license is not easy. You have to get a rather challenging undergraduate degree, work in an apprentice role for a number of years and then pass a difficult test. Engineering societies have helped establish and enhance licensing requirements in all fifty states.

There is some logic to this. We certainly want the people who design and build critical infrastructure to know what they are doing. But too often licensing is a way to protect a profession from criticism, stifle dissent, and deflect uncomfortable realities. From the Reddit thread:

> **twinnedcalcite:** ...a civil engineer could be a urban planner but an urban planner may not be an engineer or architect.
>
> **1wiseguy:** It's easy to second-guess somebody else's work when you don't actually have to take any responsibility.

Transportation engineering is, as they say, not rocket science. One does not need an engineering license to be taken seriously on any topic that would come before a local elected body, transportation issues included.

2. There Isn't Enough Money to do What Should be Done.

Project engineers work in a world where there are financial constraints. News flash: most non-engineers do as well. What makes the local municipal engineer different is that their revenue largely comes from the taxpayer. This not only frees them from some of the market constraints others must deal with but it provides a certain level of propaganda value as well.

Engineers commonly play off budget and safety against each other, as if they were two dependent variables on a sliding scale: *You can spend more and get more safety or you can spend less and get less safety....the choice is yours.* From the Reddit thread:

> **1wiseguy:** *Given enough resources, we could greatly improve safety of our streets. We could provide barriers between streets, bike lanes, and sidewalks, and provide pedestrian and bike bridges to avoid crosswalks. We could also slow traffic down arbitrarily to meet whatever safety goal we have in mind. But we don't have enough resources to build those structures, and the citizens don't want to drive slowly. What we have is deemed to be the best solution, barring occasional problems that can be addressed.*

> **Amadeus3698:** *The money is something over which the engineer has no control; the state/county/city*

government does. Blaming engineering for fiscal problems caused by elected officials shows a poor understanding of how roads are built. Petition your representatives to fund roads and tragedies like this will go away!

The notion that we are not able to design streets that are safe unless we have bloated budgets is false. That it is widely believed within the engineering profession anyway reveals a lack of innovation and a certain level of myopic comfort engineers wrongly enjoy.

3. We Can't Eliminate All Risks.

The straw man argument is standard for anyone proceeding without intellectual rigor. With the odd exception, the public does not have an expectation that all risks can be eliminated. There is an odd incoherence, however, with a profession that designs breakaway poles (they give way when struck by a vehicle) and then places said poles in a sidewalk designed to be used by people outside of a vehicle. Are vehicles leaving the roadway a threat or not? From the Reddit thread:

> **bobroberts7441:** *Any engineer could design a system that is perfectly safe; Nobody would build it. Safety is one of many constraints in any design which must first satisfy feasibility, cost, and functionality. Safety, aesthetics, environmental impact, etc. are all addressed after those are achieved and if a successful accommodation is not reached nothing gets built.*

> **Borgiedude:** *Cities collect a finite amount of tax that pays for a limited number of roadworks, upgrades and improvements. A council engineer will try and ensure those funds are spent in the way that minimizes the*

potential loss of life (save the most lives for the least money), but eliminating loss of life is financially impossible.

Transportation engineers go to enormous lengths to improve safety for those operating a vehicle. Asking them to equally consider those not in a vehicle is not asking for all risks to be eliminated. Considering the mismatch of auto versus pedestrian, it's not even leveling the playing field.

4. It is the Politicians that are to Blame. Engineers Just Follow Orders.

Oh yes, the Nuremberg defense. I know that characterization offends some of you but, seriously, why do we bother licensing engineers if they are just going to compromise their principles based on what politicians want them to do? From the Reddit thread:

> **roger_ranter:** *Engineering takes the political policies that are handed down, and the public budget that is alotted. Then the engineer has to make do with what he has, designing according to the priorities that are given. This guy is advocating an enormous change in public policy, which is fine. But politicians set policy, and taxpayers pay for it.*

> **Homeworld:** *He's angry at the consultants, instead of the people that set the public policy and distribute the funding. He should focus on MPOs (Metropolitan Planning Organizations), etc.*

Engineers do work in a world that often intersects with politics and public policy, but there are very few instances where engineers advocate for designs that compromise automobile performance in order to improve overall safety.

There are even fewer instances where politicians overrule engineers on safety in favor of faster speeds.

5. This Really is a Matter for Law Enforcement, not Engineering.

Many engineers are brilliant people capable of solving really complicated problems, even when that involves compensating for human error. The entire concept of forgiving design — where engineers design highways (and too often local streets) to "forgive" the common mistakes drivers make — is just one example.

When most people who drive along a local street exceed the speed limit, how can we call those people deviants? A deviant, by definition, is someone who deviates from the norm. If a high percentage of people are driving faster than what is really safe, it is the street that is giving drivers the wrong signals. *It's safe here....go ahead and drive fast.* That's a design flaw, not a law enforcement problem. From the Reddit thread:

> **billywob:** *Forgive me, but wouldn't increasing the law enforcement help in a lot of these situations? A lot of the discussion seems to be about ensuring that motorists abide by posted speeds, and pedestrians don't make stupid decisions (jaywalking, or running across traffic). I'm all about building better roads and such, however, isn't it also effective to post a patrol car or a speed trap to ensure motorists and pedestrians obey the rules of the road?*
>
> **billywob:** *It's not bad engineering that is encouraging fast or bad driving, its irresponsible drivers who continually take needless risks to shave half a minute off*

of their commute. If you establish a constant police presence, drivers will drive more responsibly, and THEN you can see if your road is as efficient as it was designed to be. What is more expensive, paying for a few extra shifts from cops, or building a new road that drivers are going to abuse anyways?

Why should police department budgets be stretched (or city coffers be enhanced by fines) because the engineer has designed the street incorrectly?

CONCLUSION

It is only human to resist change, particularly for those who enjoy a certain amount of entrenched power and immunity for their actions. I can forgive my fellow professional engineers for being human, but none of us should accept these deflections of criticism.

When constructing a street, engineers are taught to identify the design speed and volume and then go to the design manual to get the safe design before determining the cost.

I've queried audiences all over the country and always get the same response. The thousands of people I've asked always say that safety comes first, then cost and only then traffic volume and finally speed.

For regular people, speed is always the lowest priority, yet for professional engineers it is the first criteria upon which all other decisions rest.

It is time society asserted its values and engineers stopped imposing theirs.

Strong Towns

DESIGN MATTERS

60+mph — Safe

30-50mph — Deadly

15mph — Safe

17. THE LEAST DUMB IDEA THAT CONSENSUS PROVIDES
by Charles Marohn

(April 20, 2015) If you're reading this book, you likely know the narrative we apply to capital investments. Projects coming from the top down tend to be orderly but dumb while projects coming from the bottom up tend to be chaotic but smart. We all prefer smart to dumb, but we Americans also strongly prefer — and have established systems that enable bureaucrats and elected officials to ensure — that we get orderly over chaotic, even when it means accepting dumb as a result.

A recent example of some chaotic street art is a case in point. When I shared a story on our social media feeds about a rogue project to decorate manhole covers, even members of our audience gave some pushback. *People can't just go painting flowers on manhole covers.* The notion offends our affluent sensibilities, perceptions of our success that begin and end with the orderliness of the world around us.

I've also pointed out that it is really difficult for local

governments — even those desperate for innovation — to embrace a chaotic but smart approach, because we — American society — have little tolerance for the chaos and failure of experimentation. We accept a beta version of the next iTunes with all of its flaws to be worked out, but government had better deliver flawlessly on its promises (and with the money they already have).

Enter the megaproject; the least-dumb idea that consensus provides.

A recent article in the New Yorker on megaprojects is a treasure trove of quotes.[lxxviii] Americans scoff at the lonely bureaucrat tasked with painting crosswalks or fixing sidewalks — so little glamour in such modest work — but we culturally admire those who dream big and, like a finely pruned peacock, display the confidence commensurate with their vision. From the article:

> *Engineers are delighted to develop new technology, politicians revel in the visibility they reap from building monuments to themselves, and everyone else—developers, bankers, lawyers, consultants, landowners, contractors, and construction workers—is happy to claim a share.*[lxxix]

And unlike the beta version of iTunes and the software patch that follows, megaprojects are designed to excuse their own failures. According to the article, nine out of ten go over time and over budget. The story of Pakistan's Tarbela Dam is the example they use. Unanticipated delays intersecting with unexpectedly high inflation rates quadrupled the cost. Those things, however, are deemed beyond the control of project advocates, so no lessons are learned:

> *"Time is like a window through which black swans can fly,"* Ansar told me, alluding to the so-called black-swan theory, which explains how unexpected events shape history. *"The bigger the window, the more likely the birds fly in."*[lxxx]

I love this reference to the patron saint of Strong Towns Thinking, Nassim Taleb, and the notion of a black swan. The "theory" (it is actually more of an observation) is not that unexpected events shape history, but that we humans believe we know more than we actually do, that we can look at all the white swans around us, know that for thousands of years we've only seen white swans and then confidently conclude that all swans are white. Our hubris prevents us from not just anticipating a black swan but from even acknowledging that there are things we can't anticipate.

Doing so — acknowledging our limitations — would shatter our sense of being able to bring order to chaos in the same way Hurricane Katrina did in 2004 and, more close to home for me, flooding in the Red River Valley did back in 1997. We look back at those events as failures of systems — we didn't build the dike high enough, strong enough and thick enough — as opposed to failures of imagination; we didn't consider that we could be wrong and so we felt confident building in areas historically devastated by flood and hurricane.

This failure to be honest with ourselves — to believe there is order when there is actually just suppressed chaos — allows others to be dishonest with us. Our preference for the order of the megaproject creates opportunities for politicians, bureaucrats, corporations and labor unions to create a nice glide path for these projects to follow. From the article:

> *He [Flyvbjerg] writes that megaproject planners are*

> *often outright dishonest, systematically overestimating benefits and underestimating costs. He cites an unusually candid comment that Willie Brown, a former speaker of the California State Assembly and mayor of San Francisco, made in a 2013 newspaper column. Referring to huge cost overruns during the construction of San Francisco's four-and-a-half-billion-dollar Transbay Transit Center, Brown wrote, "We always knew the initial estimate was way under the real cost.... If people knew the real cost from the start, nothing would ever be approved. The idea is to get going. Start digging a hole and make it so big, there's no alternative to coming up with the money to fill it in."*[lxxxi]

Don't be offended by this; we actually prefer it this way.

So what is the alternative? What does chaotic but smart look like? Our friend, former Mayor of Seattle Michael McGinn, gives a rough sense of what this approach means. In referencing the Big Bertha tunneling project, the most recent poster child for failed megaprojects, the article states:

> *In 2009, McGinn, a Sierra Club activist with little political experience and modest financial backing, was elected mayor of Seattle. He had campaigned against the tunnel, arguing for a cheaper option: a plan, already found feasible by an advisory council of city and state stakeholders, to develop the city's light rail, expand bus service, and repair and reorganize streets.*
>
> *"McGinn's approach would have meant a lot of trial and error. That would all be really messy with lots of uncertainty."*[lxxxii]

Feasible, but messy. McGinn's approach would have meant

a lot of trial and error. It would also have meant some uncertainty in how traffic patterns, and subsequent investment, would adapt to the removal of the elevated highway. Changes would ultimately be needed to zoning codes, tax systems, street standards and other approaches of government to respond to an evolving reality. Today these changes would be unknown, unpredictable, because they would be incremental reactions to conditions as they happened. Some of the changes would be bad; they just wouldn't work and would need to be undone or changed in some other way. This would all be really messy with lots of uncertainty and, in a word, chaotic.

Chaotic, but really smart.

Nassim Taleb has said that, in complex systems, we need to use incremental change to probe uncertainty. However, if you are personally so confident that you have no uncertainty, or if you believe that uncertainty can be overcome through better planning (or a bigger budget), Taleb's valuable insight will be lost on you. Sadly, you will most likely be part of the orderly but dumb problem systematically destroying our cities. From the article:

> *What results, Flyvbjerg says, is the "survival of the unfittest": the least deserving projects get built precisely because their cost-benefit estimates are so misleadingly optimistic.*[lxxxiii]

Admit you don't know. Embrace the chaotic but smart. Understand that a strong town is built with a thousand competing ideas instead of one master vision. A lack of resources is forcing us there anyway; let's get started now.

18. MIDDLE OF THE ROAD KENTUCKY
by Johnny Sanphillippo

(September 9, 2015) All the talk about urbanism these days is dominated by places like Brooklyn, Portland, Vancouver, and San Francisco, largely because they're prosperous and fashionable. It's so easy to dismiss them as anomalies. Defenders of suburbia are quick to say (with some justification), "Most ordinary people don't live in places like that." So let's look at a supremely middle-of-the-road small town in Kentucky.

This is the historic Main Street in Bellevue, Kentucky. The buildings are close together, they tend to have a mix of uses with shops downstairs and apartments upstairs. The business district is walkable and bikeable. It's easy and safe for older people as well as children to navigate. The majority of the shops are locally owned. And notice that not a single building is more than three stories tall. Downtown Bellevue is... charming.

It also happens to embody all the tenets promoted by the Smart Growth "coastal elite". Except Bellevue was founded in 1870 by some profoundly conservative, market-oriented families. Bellevue isn't New Urbanism. It's just plain old fashioned regular urbanism like every other town built before World War II. Its form was dictated by practical considerations based on what worked well on a tight budget. From the beginning there was a good balance of taxable private property relative to the public cost of providing quality municipal services.

The majority of the homes in Bellevue are fully detached single family houses with front and back yards. Bellevue happens to have de facto "affordable housing" in the form of those apartments above the shops downtown and modest single family homes mixed in with the grander places in the same neighborhood. Landlords are likely to live in the same building or very nearby and to attend the same church and shop in the same stores as tenants. There's simply no need for subsidized housing or government "projects".

And Bellevue is a NORC – a Naturally Occurring Retirement Community. People just automatically like living in town in their later years. Why move to a segregated village for the elderly in Florida or Arizona with a shuttle bus to the mall on Tuesdays when you could live close to family and friends in your hometown?

Yet, Bellevue is also an excellent place for young families with children. In short, Bellevue is a complete place and an excellent example of really good urbanism that's every bit as solid as the trendy places that get all the lime light these days. Not coincidentally, its a highly sought after place to live.

Image from Google Maps[lxxxiv]

Here's something else you see in a lot of older places. Some of the best land in town along the river has been set aside as a public park. In part this is a response to the fact that the Ohio River floods periodically. Having a park take the brunt of the damage is more cost effective than building and maintaining a massive levee. But the riverside park does something else. The public park raises the collective value of all private property in town, not just expensive homes right on the water. This isn't some communist redistribution of income. It's a pragmatic capitalist technique to take a little strip of public land and passively leverage it to create much larger private value.

This photo is also from Bellevue, Kentucky. It was taken in the modern, post World War II suburban section of town next to the highway. The needs of motorists are paramount here. The streets are extra wide and there's plenty of free off-street parking. The shops cater to people who drive. The gas stations, auto parts store, car wash, supermarket, and drive-thru restaurants are all exceptionally welcoming and useful to folks in cars.

Some people like living in a walkable neighborhood. Other people prefer a driveable, suburban living arrangement. It's a big country so there's room for everyone to find a place they really love and want to call home. But there are inherent benefits and drawbacks to each kind of development. Notice that everything that makes the old part of Bellevue pleasant for people on foot makes it less conducive to people in cars. The opposite is true in the newer part of town. The more a place is made effortlessly driveable, the less it works for pedestrians or cyclists.

Bellevue has a grand total of 576 acres and serves a population of 5,900 people. It's contained on all sides by other municipalities as well as the river. Horizontal expansion isn't an option. Bellevue has a fixed amount of capital stock in the form of land. That's all there is to work with.

Here's how the suburban auto-oriented development pattern uses that scarce resource: A handful of one story, single use, semi-disposable buildings are scattered across a vast landscape of mostly empty parking lots. And nearly every one of these businesses is an out-of-town corporate chain that sucks money directly out of the local economy in exchange for a tiny sliver of sales and property tax. No one in Bellevue will ever see the owner of Kroger or McDonald's at church on Sunday or at the local PTA.

In contrast, here's a section of Bellevue's historic business district. The traditional development pattern delivers far more value per acre while requiring infinitely less public infrastructure. These small mixed use buildings from the late 1800's are as solid as ever. Because they're small and lack giant parking lagoons they tend to repel national chains that need more space and have very specific design parameters. That's actually a good thing since it creates a niche for local merchants who are far better at recirculating money within town.

Most municipalities and states (and the federal government for that matter) are consistently spending more than they collect in revenue. A majority of towns are already deep in debt and servicing that debt is becoming a larger and larger portion of the budget. The usual conversation of, "Teachers are paid way too much" and, "We just need to entice a big employer to our town" or, "If we widened the highway the new Target and Walmart will arrive to provide tax revenue" has entered an era of diminishing returns. This approach isn't going to fix what's broken. In fact, this set of policies is what's slowly destroying our towns.

The idea that compact, mixed use, pedestrian friendly development is somehow alien to American families or productive capitalism is so strange. It's exactly this type of building that made America financially and culturally strong from the very beginning. It's actually all the low grade, scattershot construction smeared across the landscape that's concentrating wealth into fewer and fewer distant hands and impoverishing ordinary towns and families.

All photographs by Johnny Sanphillippo unless otherwise noted.

19. MOVING THE OVERTON WINDOW
by Daniel Herriges

(July 30, 2015) Strong Towns has developed a cogent, powerful critique of the dysfunctional way in which cities in North America have pursued growth—a ruinous, Ponzi-scheme model of growth—for the last 70 years. And the Strong Towns website and accompanying comments have played host to much discussion of promising alternative models based on incremental development, building on a community's existing strengths, focusing on productive human-scale places, and eschewing "too-big-to-fail" investments in favor of small-scale trial and error.

And yet, I know many of us feel frustrated that the existing system just keeps barreling full-throttle toward the cliff of insolvency. It's easy to win small policy victories here and there. But even with increasing evidence that there is nationwide momentum toward walkable urbanism and away from low-returning auto-oriented development, there are few signs of the kind of fundamental, transformative change that Strong Towns has consistently argued is needed. This is particularly true when it comes to *how* we develop (and finance development), not just *what* we develop.

So how do we, as Strong Towns advocates, tip the scales? I'd like to offer some thoughts, aimed not at providing a satisfying answer to that question (not sure I have one), but more at opening up some discussion about how this movement can grow into a transformative force.

THE OVERTON WINDOW

In the ever-thrilling world of punditry and armchair political science, there's a concept called the Overton Window, which has attracted some attention and analysis in recent years. (This is not to be confused with the universally and entertainingly panned Glenn Beck novel based on said concept.) Coined in the 1990s by Joseph Overton of the Mackinac Center, a libertarian-leaning think tank, the Overton Window represents the range of policy positions on a given issue that are broadly considered acceptable, mainstream, and nonthreatening.

The Overton Window usually corresponds to the set of policies that elected officials will be willing to advocate and go to bat for—which is inevitably much smaller than the set of all possible policy solutions to a given problem. To either side of the window are views that, while they may have significant popular support, a politician seeking reelection is likely to deem too "extreme" to stake his or her career on.

If the conceivable policy options on an issue can be expressed on some sort of continuum (which can take many forms, not just left vs. right), there is likely an identifiable Overton Window.

For example, here's a possible urbanism-related Overton

Window, in this case placing policies related to bike infrastructure on a continuum of extremely pro-cycling vs. extremely anti-cycling:

Cars banned from many or all streets
Comprehensive network of segregated bike infrastructure citywide
Protected bikeways on major corridors citywide
Protected bikeways in select corridors with high bike traffic
Reduce car lanes in some cases to accommodate bike lanes
> Painted bike lanes where possible without taking space from cars
> Painted bike lanes only on a handful of high-demand streets
> No bike lanes, but sharrows and "share the road with bicycles" signs
> No bike infrastructure or signage
Bicycles banned from streets with busy car traffic
Bicycles banned from many or all streets

Now, let's say that for one reason or another, the city or metro region depicted above sees a massive increase over the span of a few years in public support for cycling as a transportation option, and for infrastructure to make cycling safe and comfortable. Perhaps the window shifts in the pro-biking direction, like this:

Cars banned from many or all streets
Comprehensive network of segregated bike infrastructure citywide
> Protected bikeways on major corridors citywide
> Protected bikeways in select corridors with high bike traffic
> Reduce car lanes in some cases to accommodate bike lanes
> Painted bike lanes where possible without taking space from cars
Painted bike lanes only on a handful of high-demand streets
No bike lanes, but sharrows and "share the road with bicycles" signs
No bike infrastructure or signage
Bicycles banned from streets with busy car traffic
Bicycles banned from many or all streets

If, as Otto von Bismarck once said, politics is "the art of the possible," the Overton Window represents the limits of the—currently—possible. Shifting that window, then, becomes the task of the activist. An important point is that politicians themselves are rarely the ones to do it, as the Mackinac Center's own Joseph Lehman observes:

> *In our understanding, politicians typically don't determine what is politically acceptable; more often, they react to it and validate it. Generally speaking, policy change follows political change, which itself follows social change. The most durable policy changes are those that are undergirded by strong social movements.*[lxxxv]

There is an important implication here: if you want to create massive change, you shouldn't necessarily focus on convincing elected officials. They're hamstrung by what they perceive as the acceptable center of public opinion, because, like all of us, they would prefer to keep their jobs.

THE PERCEIVED CENTER

"People here will never give up their cars." How many times have you heard that assertion, or some close relative of it?

Aside from the obnoxious straw-man aspect—nobody, not the most diehard urbanist, is actually out to forcibly take away anyone's car—statements like that are really expressions of where the speaker perceives the limits of the local urbanism Overton Window to be. Sure, maybe cycling is huge in Copenhagen or Amsterdam, and maybe even the rich use transit in Tokyo or London. But that's *there*. This is *here*. We couldn't ever do that *here*.

Urbanists like to get indignant at the irrationality of policymakers who don't do what we want them to do. We spend our time reading about best practices, and we know how much more pleasant—and how much more fiscally productive—urban environments can be when built at the human scale instead of the automobile scale. We know this. We have *empirical evidence*, dammit. Plus, have you ever *been* to Europe? Hell, even New Orleans, Savannah, or Quebec City? And besides, urbanism is trendy nowadays. Every city that matters is in an arms race to attract "creative class" millennials with bike lanes, parklets, coffee and craft beer. How can they not *get it*? Sarcasm aside, I know I often feel this way.

If you communicate with your elected officials, they probably use at least some of the right buzzwords. The planning staff, at least the younger ones, probably have their hearts in the right place. And then they go and disregard everything that we know — *they* know — they should be doing, doubling down on stroad design and touting their new, shiny diverging diamond freeway interchanges.

The key is that the "art of the possible" is not a matter of which policies are rational. It's not even a matter of which policies are actually "moderate" in their ultimate impact. It's simply which policies are *perceived* to be acceptably mainstream in the local context, rightly or wrongly.

This perception can result from all sorts of illogical ideas.

In July of 2015, Human Transit's Jarrett Walker shared a video of a fantastic presentation he did in Portland.[lxxxvi] In it, he talks about our tendency to underestimate the rationality of other people's actions — attributing them to culture or highly subjective preferences instead. "We've all heard that

Los Angeles has a car culture," he says, but LA doesn't have a "car culture." LA has an urban form and infrastructure in which most people are making the rational choice to meet their travel needs by driving.

And yet the perception of a car culture does limit the Overton Window for LA urban policymakers. Not intractably—in fact, LA has made impressive progress in some places toward a more productive and human-scale development model, more so in recent years than some American cities far more renowned for their urbanism and walkability. What matters for policy is that a significant number of Angelenos *believe* that LA has a car culture. A significant number of LA elected officials may be hesitant to endorse policies perceived as a direct challenge to that "car culture." The status quo becomes self-reinforcing.

MOVING THE WINDOW FROM OUTSIDE

One key insight about the Overton Window is that it's most readily moved from the outside. No one is very threatened by tinkering within the mainstream, so such tinkering doesn't provoke a dramatic response. It takes an effective, radical critique to shake up the public discourse on a subject. And when such a critique is successful, change is often breathtakingly rapid.

It's why gay rights organizations consciously decided to push for full same-sex marriage and not settle for civil unions or some other legal arrangement. Staking out a position that could have been accommodated without upending then-mainstream conceptions of the state's role in marriage offered limited returns. Staking out an inherently transformative position, one that fundamentally had to change the public discourse to be successful—well, we've now seen how that worked out. The Overton Window of gay rights has lurched to a new position, and it's not going back.

The Overton Window exists in part because of a widespread cognitive bias people have toward triangulating "moderate" as the average of two positions they perceive as "extreme." Our brains love mental shortcuts when it comes to evaluating new ideas, and this is an easy one to take. This means that public exposure for a radical position on an issue can shift the window by creating room for other views to appear moderate by comparison. If you grab one end of the window and stretch it, the center moves too.

This is why mainstream Republican politicians (the GOP has always been more aware of the Overton Window than the Democrats, and better at using it to their advantage) love it when guys like Rush Limbaugh and Bill O'Reilly say shocking things that rile up the base, so they can reap the benefits both of the riled-up base and of appearing composed and reasonable in contrast.

Radicalism as a means of moving the window has been the approach of the National Rifle Association to its advocacy against gun control and — any opinions on its actual policy positions aside — it's indisputable that the NRA is one of the most astonishingly successful advocacy organizations of all time. With a nationwide member base millions strong, the NRA has established a lock on one end of the gun control discourse, and it dictates where that end is.

On the left side of the spectrum, the recent viral success of the Black Lives Matter movement seems to be a case of moving the Overton Window on issues involving law enforcement accountability and institutional racism. (Note: I am *not* in any way suggesting that the idea itself—that black lives matter, or that racism is endemic in institutions including the police—is radical or "extreme." I am just observing that the window seems to have shifted in response to a social movement, to the point where mainstream politicians can say things they would not have said even a decade ago.)

So, Strong Towns advocates who would like to see not merely a bike lane here and a traffic-calming project there, but a full-blown end to the Suburban Experiment and a return to tried-and-true methods of building fiscally sustainable, resilient cities: What do you think a successful viral campaign or social movement with this goal will look like?

THE FALLACY OF "WORK WITHIN THE SYSTEM WE HAVE" POLITICS

I am all for the #NoNewRoads hashtag that Strong Towns has been pushing. And yet, I don't actually believe that there should not, anywhere, under any circumstances, be new roads built. And I absolutely don't think that's a politically viable outcome. That's not the point. The point is doing what we can to spark a transformative change in the public discourse.

For this, I've seen Strong Towns, and often Chuck Marohn personally, called "angry," "off-putting," "strident," "negative," "not constructive," and many other things of that sort. This criticism misses the point.

One of the most acrimonious debates I've seen in urbanist circles of late has been over whether to support or oppose massive infrastructure spending campaigns in order to reap the transit and/or multimodal benefits. One such proposal, from the MoveMN coalition in Minnesota, inspired a point and subsequent Strong Towns counterpoint piece on the Minnesota urbanist blog, Streets.MN. I won't delve into it in any depth, but the crux of the issue is that transit, bike, and pedestrian project funding is often tied to these proposals, and for those who want to see such projects move forward, it can become a matter of begging for table scraps because it is scraps or nothing.

And yet, if you work within the dysfunctional political process and funding mechanisms we have to get what you want this time, what about next time? What about the time after that?

There may be valid reasons to ultimately support an organization like MoveMN. It's a difficult issue and one about which I'm conflicted. But let's not pretend it's a stepping stone to real change. It will do nothing to move the Overton Window in the direction of saner infrastructure policy. And sooner or later, if we keep doing what we've been doing, we *will* run out of money.

Let the politicians practice the art of the possible. As advocates, our job is to talk about what *should* be possible—and to make a compelling case for it until it catches on and spreads.

That doesn't mean we shouldn't be pragmatic in our coalition-building, or on specific issues where there's a near-term chance to get something done. Rather, it means we shouldn't let the pragmatic be the enemy of the transformative.

WHERE TO NOW?

Online organizer Josh Bolotsky at Beautiful Trouble puts it nicely:

> *Not all radical positions are effective in shifting the Overton window, so don't just reach for any old radical idea. Ideally, the position you promote should carry logical and moral force, and must include some common ground with your own position — it needs to be along the same continuum of belief if it is to be effective. It also must not be so far out of the mainstream that it becomes toxic for anyone vaguely associated with it, or the backlash will in fact push the Window in the opposite of the desired direction.*[lxxxvii]

Are we seeing this backlash against urbanism in certain political contexts? In the allegations of a "War on Cars" that seem to spring up whenever any city makes steps toward reclaiming public space from the automobile? Personally, I doubt it—especially given the remarkably innocuous and inconsequential nature of some of the policies that seem to be enough to trigger "War on cars!" hysteria. I suspect this is better read as a sign that the old guard is losing and we're—not quickly enough, but surely—gaining ground.

How can Strong Towns be effective in transforming the discourse about how we build cities? What positions should we stake out that are outside the current mainstream but backed by compelling evidence and moral reasoning? How should we frame them to have the best chance of gaining viral momentum?

Where, on an issue you care about, are there signs of a shift in the window already complete or in progress? What positions are tenable or even totally uncontroversial now that would have been seen as radical or untenable 20 years ago? For example, I'd suggest the fact that New York City's pedestrianizing of Times Square has been a smashing success, yet nobody could have envisioned it as recently as the 1990s. And just this summer, Minneapolis did away with some—sadly not all—of its mandatory parking minimums. Small steps, but signs of change.

Progress in concrete form—in a given community, on a given project—may be one step forward, two steps back. But the pace of social change is nonlinear—the stunning snowball effect of the gay marriage movement is proof of that. If we can help shift the Overton Window and open up new avenues for policymakers, it's a different ballgame.

Strong Towns

Photo courtesy of Jonathan Holth

20. MY CAR PAYS CHEAPER RENT THAN ME
by Andrew Price

(November 23, 2015) The title of this chapter is catchy, except, to be honest, I do not own a car anymore. We sold our car when we moved to Hoboken, NJ. My wife and I both commute to Manhattan, and we are spoiled with trains, buses, and ferries. When we stick around Hoboken, we walk to restaurants, to parks, to church. Much of Hoboken's charm comes from the city being only 1.3 square miles, so pretty much the entire city of Hoboken is within walking distance. Occasionally we want to go off the beaten path and head into more suburban parts of New Jersey, and have used Uber (our average Uber trip costs around $10), but after living here for nearly 4 months, we've used Uber a total of 7 times. All of that combined is cheaper than just one month of what we were paying for car insurance.

My point in telling you this is that Hoboken is one of the few places in the United States where not owning a car does not feel like a hindrance. In fact, this was a major selling point for us, and probably for a lot of other people (because the rent is incredibly high which signifies that there is a lot of demand to live here.) And still, like many cities across the United States, we have parking minimums.

These are the questions I'd like my city leaders to answer about parking minimums:

1. Why do we have parking minimums?

Seriously, why? What was the discussion going on in city hall when they thought this was needed? Is it to compete with the suburbs? Real estate prices in Hoboken are extremely high, a sign that there is huge demand to live here. I chose to live here because it is not suburban, so why would we adopt policies that make our city more suburban? Why would we adopt ordinances that make most of our city's character illegal if we were to develop it from scratch today?

2. Who decides parking minimums?

Why do the parking regulations for Hoboken say a bowling alley requires two spaces per alley?[lxxxviii] Why not one or three? Why do "planned unit developments" require 1 space per dwelling? How did we figure out this was the optimal number?

There is a saying at Google where I work: Data is king. You can't make decisions without data, especially not ones with long term implications. I would like to see the data that states one parking space per 200 square feet (not 100 or 300) of a skating rink is optimum to bring prosperity to the city. Where is the data to show these optimal ratios before it was encoded into city law forevermore?

A parking space is around 250 square feet. If we built one

parking space per 200 square feet of skating rink, we would be dedicating more space to 'getting there' than being 'there'.

3. In an urban neighborhood where most people walk for local trips, why should local businesses be forced to accommodate cars?

95% of trips in Hoboken take place on foot.[lxxxix] So, what would people in a dense urban community like ours actually need a car for?

4. Why do we think we can act in a business's best interest better than the business?

It's within a business's best interest to make as much money as possible, which means making themselves accessible so that customers can get through the door. Let's assume that the remaining 5% of local trips are done in a car (and not on a bus or a bike). Should a business not be the one to decide if it should dedicate expensive, valuable land to accommodate that 5% of customers that might travel by car, or if it would be better to put that space to productive use and attract the remaining 95% of potential customer base that travels by foot?

Who do the parking minimums help? Not the businesses that would be forced to subsidize a very small minority of customers when they could make more money by putting that land to productive use.

5. Why do we subsidize and encourage driving?

It seems counterproductive. Hoboken is one of the few places where driving is optional; it is not necessary to have a car to get around. Every time we make it easier to walk, ride a bicycle, or use transit, more people will do so. Likewise, the easier to own or drive a car, the more people that will do so. Arguments that "we need to make it easier to drive, because we predict more people will drive" become self-fulling prophecies because they cause us to adopt policies that end up inducing people to drive. The city has initiatives to encourage residents not to drive,[xc] yet we cancel them out with our parking regulations.

6. Why should my car pay cheaper rent than me?

In Hoboken, an on-street parking permit is $15 per year, or $1.25 per month.[xci] A typical garage parking space costs about $300 per month. Let's assume an average parking space is 250 square feet.[xcii] Housing a car on the street costs $0.03/square foot/month, and housing a car in a garage costs $1.20/square foot/month. In contrast, housing a human in Hoboken averages around $3.25/square foot/month (at the time of writing.)[xciii]

Hoboken has an affordable housing problem.[xciv] Having shelter is a basic human right while housing a car is not. Why does it cost a person 108 times more (per square foot) to house themselves over their car?

A small living structure or tent could replace maybe 2 parking spaces. I am not implying that we should start building parking-space sized homes on our streets, but I am pointing out the real inequality we get from subsidizing car housing over human housing, both in the public and private realms.

A parking space in Hoboken would average around $812.50/month if housing a car per square foot matched housing a person. Naturally, housing a car is going to be a little cheaper because a car doesn't ask for plumbing and air conditioning and the space requires little ongoing maintenance. But, let's say you had floor space in a building and wanted to get the highest return out of your investment and you wanted to get as much revenue per square foot as possible. Not many people are going to pay $800/month for a parking space. I imagine that is why these large apartment complexes, that were required by zoning to provide parking, are renting the spaces for $300/month, in order to get enough demand to rent them out. But, we have a housing shortage, so if given the choice, would the building owners have preferred the floor space of their building making 2.7x per square foot as apartments instead of parking spaces? In effect, parking minimums are forcing property owners to take a loss.

In the cities I have looked at, it is substantially cheaper to house a car (a luxury item) per square foot than a human (a basic human right.) Here are the most expensive major American cities in which to rent a monthly parking space:[xcv]
- New York - $541/month
- Boston - $438/month
- San Francisco - $375/month
- Philadelphia - $303/month
- Seattle - $294/month

Why are our cars paying cheaper rent than us?

7. What is stopping us from eliminating parking minimums?

Hope is not lost. We can repeal our parking minimums, and go back to building great fine-grained urban places that people love, that put our valuable and limited land to productive use, and will make our city economically resilient and financially stronger. Regulating something just for the sake of regulating it is an orderly but dumb approach. If people want parking, let them pay for it. To force businesses to take a loss to subsidize parking when we have a housing shortage is unnecessary and harmful. It is time for the United States' most walkable city[xcvi] to join the list of cities that have eliminated parking minimums.[xcvii]

*For more on parking minimums,
check out our annual #BlackFridayParking event:*

www.strongtowns.org/blackfridayparking

21. I'M NOT AFRAID
by Charles Marohn

(November 30, 2015) Last week, I finally got the roof on my house fixed. It was damaged in a severe storm in July, a mini-disaster in my life that came at a very difficult time. We had just finished a new strategic plan here at Strong Towns and I was in the middle of a staff transition. I was trying to hire two people — with tons of conflicting advice on how to go about it — and we were having serious member retention issues. I was also not keeping up with the content stream on our website and was hearing from some of our members about that. And, at the end of the summer, I knew I was going to be heading out on the road for ten weeks straight. Not the best time to have four trees dropped on your house.

In addition to these work stresses, my home life was a challenge: Not only was my roof damaged but we had sheetrock and carpet that had then gotten rained on. My shady yard full of oak trees and leafy shrubs was now a scene of devastation. My oldest daughter was going to be attending a new school on a big campus way out of town and

I could go on, but I'll spare my family members and allow us our privacy. Let's just say it was quite a stressful time.

Having a roof over my head now that doesn't leak — getting rid of the buckets and the towels — feels like a bit of a luxury. As we sat down for our Thanksgiving meal, I felt we had a lot to be thankful for. Nobody died and, besides some scrapes, sore muscles and an episode with a bees nest, nobody was hurt all that much. The carpet and ceiling should be fixed by Christmas. The yard will take a while but it will grow back. We're lucky.

Those of you that know me or have followed me on Facebook or Twitter likely know that I've struggled with the direction our national dialog took in late 2015 on the issue of Syrian refugees in general and the Muslim religion in specific. While we do talk about community, neighbors and Strong Citizens here, I've not brought up the refugee issue at Strong Towns very often, largely because of how intertwined it has become with our politics. Strong Towns is not a political organization, we have no political leanings and, in fact, have a really broad group of political affiliations among our staff, board and members. For an issue that is not central to who we are, I just opted to stay away from it.

As I pick up the buckets and put away the towels, as I ponder the gifts I wish to buy for my daughters, family and friends over the next few weeks, as I sit with my belly full and my feet warm, I can't help but return to this issue.

I keep pondering a statement someone recently shared with me on social media:

> *If only we had a seasonally-appropriate story about Middle Eastern people seeking refuge being turned away*

by the heartless.

If only....

The central insight of Strong Towns is that our post World War II development pattern was a huge experiment. It created an illusion of wealth, one that we have tried to sustain with warped economic policy derived from convenient economic theory. We're in the process of seeing that illusion destroyed and, with it, much of our national identity vis-a-vis the rest of the world (aka: the American dream).

As we study civilizations that have gone through resets such as the one we are attempting to navigate, there are success stories and there are tragedies. England after World War II, which lost its entire global empire yet retained its bearings and, thus, its influence on the world stage, is what I would call a success story. Japan of that same time period could be similarly classified. Germany after World War I, however, went a completely different way. You could say the same about the last decades of czarist Russia, the Soviet Union under Stalin and Mao's China.

Transition is a time of uncertainty. As Nassim Taleb would suggest, this is even more so when you add layers of fragility to a system — debt, energy dependency, globalized trade — that create cascading inter-dependencies. I just finished the book *Asia's Cauldron: The South China Sea and the End of a Stable Pacific* by Robert Kaplan. You think we or China would risk a devastating war over a few submerged atolls in the South China Sea? No, but would you think Germany would risk a devastating war with their major trading partners England and France over the assassination of an archduke from a neighboring, crumbling empire?

Times of desperation magnify our insecurities and leave us collectively prone to shameful conduct. We're appalled — we can't imagine what they were even thinking — that people who looked like, and may have been ethnically similar to, the people who bombed our naval base at Pearl Harbor in 1941 were put into internment camps over the course of the subsequent war. Yet our national discourse today includes allusions to doing the same with people who look like, and may be ethnically similar to, the people who attacked us on 9/11. The German conversation during the 1930's regarding Jews began in a similar way.

This is because humans are flawed. In Maslow's hierarchy of needs, security is far more important than friendship, self-esteem and even morality. The words of Hermann Goering at the Nuremberg trials resonate throughout time because they are horrifically true:

> *Voice or no voice, the people can always be brought to the bidding of the leaders. That is easy. All you have to do is tell them they are being attacked, and denounce the peacemakers for lack of patriotism and exposing the country to danger. It works the same in any country.*[xcviii]

My biggest fear for our country is that, as we go through this transition — one where I think we go from Americans living in unrivaled prosperity to merely well above world average — we lose who we are. We cease striving to be better people. We accept a position of diminished moral leadership both here and abroad. I think that world would be a darker place.

One of America's great virtues is that we have historically been a home for the oppressed, for those seeking refuge. Go to any major city in the eastern part of this country and experience the ethnic neighborhoods, be they Irish or German or Jewish. These people didn't move here and then *assimilate*. They came as collective waves and they clung to each other, their own identity and their own customs as they made their way in this strange new place. Yet, over time, the opportunity afforded them here prompted them not to *assimilate* but to *integrate*, to combine with Americans to become a greater whole.

I'm a Catholic. In the past, Catholic immigrants were not trusted to be real Americans. They had strange beliefs about communion bread and wine. Some said they owed their allegiance to the Pope and could not be trusted. It was also suggested that Irish Catholics in particular would be terrorists (and some did ship weapons and give financial support to the IRA back in Ireland, but we weren't overrun with terrorism). They took low paying jobs which "drove down wages". You can take our dialog back a century, replace "Muslim" with "Catholic" and you would hardly know the difference.

There is a difference, however. Those refugees of the past were entering a country in ascension, one where our cities were strong and becoming stronger, where jobs and growth and economic opportunity were a byproduct of things we collectively did together at the local level. It was the perfect place for someone used to hardship to bootstrap themselves to a better life.

Our affluence — that illusion of wealth — has moved us a long ways from that hungrier existence. Like the rich kid whose trust fund is running low, our world — while still incredibly privileged — is about to get a little harder. We can actually learn a lot from integrating some fresh blood into our national body. I think refugees — much like artists and other traditionally marginalized members of society —

are a key catalyst for moving us back into a Strong Towns way of being.

Either way, I'm not afraid. You should not be either.

22. THE DENSITY QUESTION
by Charles Marohn

(March 29, 2015) The most common question I receive by email is some variation of: What is the right density for a Strong Town? What is the magic number that makes all the math work, the ratios we should plug into our zoning codes to get the optimum place?

The act of asking such a question indicates to me that the sender (a) has not read much of our work or (b) has read Strong Towns but not spent much time thinking about it. Either way, in the extreme triage that is my inbox, these emails rank pretty low.

Just before I went on vacation, a colleague sent me another version of one of these emails and suggested, based on the number of times it has been asked, that I give it another go. Here's the specific question this time:

> *Something that I think would be valuable for planners and everyone else, is to have a reference for how to build financially solvent towns at varying levels of*

> *density/size. What is the right kind of infrastructure for a town of 5000 with 800 people/sq mi, versus a town of 15000 with 2000 people/sq mi?*

Let me restate the question:

> *Something that I think would be valuable for planners and everyone else who finds it painful to think independently but prefer instead to take comfort in misapplying "data" provided by others deemed experts (see parking codes as one of many examples) is to have a table of densities that will allow us to zone a Strong Town.*

I hate density as a metric. Whenever I hear someone talk about it my mind reflexively moves on to something more worthy of my time. Yours should too. Density is not our problem or our solution. Insolvency is our problem. Productive places are the solution.

Anyone who remotely comprehends the number of variables at play here would never ask such a ridiculous question. How valuable are the units? How well is the street maintained? What is the inflation rate for construction costs? What is the city's bond rating? Will the association properly maintain the roof of the building? What will happen to the building across the street currently in probate? Does the city's code empower NIMBY's?

I could go on and on and on.... If density matters for anything, it is a byproduct of success, not its cause. And I'm not even sold on that.

Here's how we should be thinking about this. Consider the following: You own a $200,000 house. I come to you on behalf of the city with a proposal. We are going to fix all of the infrastructure directly in front of your home. We're going to fix the street and the curb and the sidewalk. We're going to replace all the pipes and service connections. And when we're done with this project, a once-a-generation undertaking – we're going to give you the bill.

And when we give you the bill for the stuff that directly serves you – the stuff that only you need – we're going to also give you a bill for your share of the communal infrastructure. In other words, you are going to also pay a once-a-generation charge for the maintenance and upkeep of all the arterial streets, interchanges, traffic signals, lift station pumps, water towers, treatment facilities, etc… It will only be your share – everyone else will pay theirs – and you won't be billed again for a generation.

Remember that you own a $200,000 house. What if I said your total bill was $200,000? Would you pay it? I've been asking people this exact question for the past two weeks and have yet to encounter anyone who didn't immediately say, "No, there is no way." And, of course, nobody would pay this. If the house is worth $200,000 and my additional cost of maintaining the infrastructure to allow me to live in that house for the next three decades is an additional $200,000, then that's a really bad investment.

What if I said your total bill was $100,000; half the value of your house. Again, everyone I asked this question to would give up their house and look somewhere else before shouldering this bill. And even if you are not one, all your neighbors would be, which would spell the end of your neighborhood.

So how about a $20,000 bill? Now we're starting to get into the "it depends" range. If you had no equity in the home, then you're almost guaranteed to walk. If, on the other hand, you own the house clear and free, then you've got some incentive to suck it up and pay, albeit grudgingly.

It is only when I got to $10,000 where people in large numbers would agree they would pay and, at $5,000, I started to get universal acceptance. For a $200,000 house, it is definitely worth an additional investment of $5,000 to keep all the basic infrastructure around it functioning.

I think this is a reasonable thought process and it points to a powerful conclusion. At a property value to infrastructure investment ratio of 1:1, everybody walks. Nobody sensible is going to invest $200,000 in infrastructure in a property and have it end up being valued at only $200,000. What's the point?

At a ratio of 10:1, resistance starts to soften and we see people with different circumstances start to respond differently. Somewhere between 20:1 and 40:1 we cross over into no-brainer territory. Nobody is going to walk away from a $200,000 investment if all they have to put in is another $5,000 once a generation to keep it all maintained.

So instead of density, what we're really talking about here is a target ratio of private investment to public investment of somewhere between 20:1 on the risky end and 40:1 on the secure end. If your city has $40 billion of total value when you add up all private investments, sustaining public investments of $1 billion (40:1) is a very secure proposition. Public investments totaling $2 billion (20:1) starts to be risky with outside forces of inflation, interest rates and other factors beyond your control starting to impact your potential solvency.

Let me explain this a different way. If you own the Empire State Building in NYC, which is appraised at $2.5 billion, finding a few million to fix the street and pipes in front of the building is not going to impair the value of your property. It's not a deal killer. Push comes to shove, you'll make that happen. However, if you have a large acre lot with a house worth $320,000 and the city comes to you with an $80,000 bill to provide you sewer, water and an improved street (I've seen that exact scenario proposed and shot down), that's going nowhere. It doesn't make financial sense.

And, at the end of the day, we need to build cities that make financial sense.

If all of this is logical to you, let me deliver the bad news. And by "bad" know that I'm understating substantially. Let me deliver the tragic news that demonstrates why discussions of density, zoning, new highways, high speed rail across America, recreational trails, decorative lights and every other fetish of the modern planner is a sad distraction from our urgent problems. I've now done this analysis in two cities – one big and one small – and for a $200,000 house in either of these cities, the once-a-generation bill for your share of the infrastructure would be between $350,000 and $400,000.

That's right; these cities have more public investment than private investment. As we gather more data, I suspect these two examples will not be anomalies. Forget sensible ratios of 20:1 or 40:1. In pursuit of our fanatical belief that public infrastructure investment drives private investment, we have cities that have actually accumulated more public infrastructure liability than they have total private investment.

That is bizarre. There is no way all this public investment

will ever be maintained. In the coming years and decades, our cities are going to contract in ways that are foreseeable, if not specifically predictable. Yet most are still obsessed with growth and, the "progressive" among us, with issues of density.

Instead of density, here's the question that should keep you up at night: What combination of increase in private investment and downsizing of public investment will give my city a private to public investment ratio of 30:1?

If you can answer it theoretically before Detroit discovers it through trial and error, perhaps you can avoid the pain all of our cities seem destined to experience.

23. EFFICIENCY
by Charles Marohn and Ruben Anderson

(March 31, 2015) My thoughts on density led to a fascinating and distracting discussion. One exchange, in particular, about efficiency deserves some highlight.

A commenter named "Mike" was making the quintessential 1970's environmentalist argument:

> *Density is about efficiency. More tax revenue per whatever, fewer infrastructure requirements compared to sprawl, more people for efficient transit, which means fewer cars on the road, potentially, greater walkability, etc.*

I call this the 1970's environmentalist argument because this is the same argument I consistently ran into from Baby Boomers who fought for environmentalism early in life but now have the lake home in the woods (so they can enjoy the environment they fought to keep others out of)[xcix]. Their argument, when the next round of their ilk wanted to enjoy the lake, was: less is better. Three new lots are better than five. One is better than three. Less is better and, as Mike would expound on to great lengths, more is worse in that scenario.

I tried to draw out an understanding of what he meant by "efficient" because I obviously do not agree with his universal truth. That really went nowhere, but I'll give you the question I put forth as a discussion point:

> *As you define efficient, do Darwin's theories on evolution and natural selection describe a process that is or is not efficient?*

An answer to this question was not forthcoming, but my favorite all time commenter, Ruben Anderson, provided a brilliant reply that deserves its own place in the Strong Towns Canon. Here's that wisdom from Ruben:

> Mike, I will try to channel Charles here.
>
> You asked what has a "high level of adaptability, [uses] smaller amounts of resources [and] maintains the modern way of life?"
>
> It is like the old saying, "You can have this fast, cheap, or good. Pick any two,"
>
> What you are asking for cannot be done. Charles keeps asking you to give examples from evolutionary history for the simple reason that nature has done trillions upon trillions of experiments—literally every life form that has ever existed is a new, slightly modified experiment (with the exception, perhaps, of reproduction by cloning, and we could still argue that).

So, we have a history of staggering amounts of testing, compared with a tiny handful of human ideas—and yet we swagger around talking about the "efficiency" of our machines and cities and economies. We don't have a clue what we are talking about.

Adaptability and efficiency are polar opposites. If you have the resources to adapt, you have lost opportunity for "efficiency". Whether those resources are in the form of spare food, spare limbs, spare DNA, spare cultural redundancy, spare knowledge, whatever, it doesn't matter. Surplus is a resource that may not have been used in human memory, and therefore is a great candidate for "efficiency". If it is surplus, it means by definition you don't currently need it.

Until you do. You can't adapt without surplus. Surplus DNA. Surplus farmland. Surplus building space. Surplus building materials. If you have no surplus, you have nothing with which to work, and so you have no adaptability.

There have been plenty of efficient creatures in the history of this planet—most of the extinct ones. They were not adaptable to change.

So, it sure is efficient to levee the Mississippi River, such that the river bottom is actually higher than the land to either side. That is a highly fragile situation, though, that is not adaptable to changing circumstances, like a hurricane. A much more adaptable approach is to let the river move naturally, and to keep our buildings off the floodplains.

It is very efficient to build section after section of tract homes, all the same, with the same floor plan, same materials, same landscaping, same utilities. But the suburbs are not very adaptable.

The book to read on this topic is *Antifragile*, by Nassim Nicholas Taleb. And the book to read to break down the notion of nature as efficient is McDonough and Braungart's *Cradle to Cradle*.

They show that nature is not at all efficient. Think of the cherry tree that is covered with tens of thousands of blossoms that just uselessly fall on the ground. That is not very efficient.

But it is beautiful. Do we go out to nice restaurants to have an efficient meal? Do we want to efficiently make love?

No. Efficiency is what you strive for when you are doing things that are bad, and you want to do them less bad. But what we want are things that are good. Like cherry blossoms. If things are good, you can do them more good, and have more cherry blossoms.

So nature is not efficient, but it is non-toxic and fully recyclable. All those wasted blossoms go on to feed the biological nutrient cycle. McDonough and Braungart advocate we emulate nature and create a totally recyclable technical nutrient cycle—unlike our current system of almost no recyclability and wanton downcycling. If all waste is captured as a recyclable or upcyclable biological or technical nutrient then we don't need to be efficient. Waste equals food. And if you have all that surplus, you are very adaptable.

So, you asked what has a "high level of adaptability,

[uses] smaller amounts of resources [and] maintains the modern way of life?"

I have given you the resources to understand why efficiency and adaptability are opposites.

You are quite correct that we are in a bind, though. We don't build our world in a *Cradle to Cradle* way. We don't build good, we build bad, and the correct thing to do in the short term is to use efficiency to be less bad.

But if you are hoping that will extend the modern way of life, I have bad news; the modern way of life is already off the table. This shows up everywhere: cities returning roads to gravel, increasing rates of infant mortality, scraping the bottom of the barrel oil and gas fracking, dropping literacy, and lowered life expectancies. Even the Nordic Wonders, like Norway, have only built a social welfare state on the one-time bonanza of North Sea oil.

We can't efficient our way back to the modern way of life. So, we desperately need adaptability to deal with the quickly changing world we find ourselves in.

Read that again and again. It is really just perfect.

24. WHAT THE WORLD NEEDS NOW
by Gracen Johnson

(April 21, 2015) Love, folks. It's love. Love conquers all. At least that has been my almost unbearably hackneyed conclusion so far.

Last week, I was asked to join a panel discussion posed with the question: What role does placemaking have in building sustainable communities? This gave me a great excuse to break down and map out my personal theory of change. Here it is: love and working together. Have no doubt, the triteness is not lost on me - I grimace even writing this, but I really believe there's something to it.

VACUUM-DRIVEN DEVELOPMENT

I arrived in the world of regeneration and "sustainable development" with an honest-to-goodness optimism about policy-driven change. Call it institutionalism or what have you, but I believed like so many of us do that the right policies and incentives could build the world we want. My MPhil (in something called Planning, Growth, and

Regeneration) was an entire degree focused on the policies and economic tools employed in regenerating places. I still believe policy is important and essential, such as putting a price on greenhouse gas emissions and installing feedback systems like road pricing. There are housing policies and anti-policies that I can get behind, and let's not forget about parking maximums. Where my confidence falters is in the zone of traditional economic development policy, the stuff of business parks and tax perks.

The revelation occurred while attending a conference about struggling rural villages that were desperate to create jobs and retain young people. I had just been contemplating these same challenges for large cities like Liverpool, UK at school and it hit me that everyone feels like a struggling rural village in the globalized economy, except the top dogs like New York, San Francisco, Tokyo, London and Shanghai, etc.

Common practice favors what I call vacuum-driven economic development, where your goal is to suck up more talent, resources, and "job-creators" than your neighbors. We've seen all the tricks to do this, mostly resembling some form of bribery, freebies, or pleading with the government. It's naively self-interested and doesn't scale well. These policies don't work in the long-term for most of us because, no matter how much money we throw at it, we can't compete with the awesome vacuum power of the cities at the top of the food chain. Further, there are casualties to an obsession with building "competitive" cities. Aspiring to be a vacuum means endorsing the painful losses of specific communities so that others can win. And we all know life is not a level playing field.

"LOVE WILL SAVE THIS PLACE."

So I began pondering how we could create new value that is independent of the vacuums. Is there a form of value and meaning that creates an unbeatable stickiness, bound up in place? Of course there is: love. Love makes us do irrational things, like stay in a place where we need to fight tooth and nail to create opportunity for ourselves. The number of times family and memories came up when I asked my friends, "Why do you live where you live?" is testament to that.

We protect, improve, and beautify the places we love. Nowhere is this more obvious today than multi-generation farmers or the First Nations that are putting their lives on the line to protect the places they love and depend on from toxic spills and emissions. In the book, *This Changes Everything*, Naomi Klein shares the words of Montana rancher Alexis Bonogofsky:

> It sounds ridiculous but there's this one spot where I can sit on the sandstone rock and you know that the mule deer are coming up and migrating through, you just watch these huge herds come through, and you know that they've been doing that for thousands and thousands of years. And you sit there and you feel connected to that. And sometimes it's almost like you can feel the earth breathe. That connection to this place and the love that people have for it, that's what Arch Coal doesn't get. They underestimate that. They don't understand it so they disregard it. And that's what in the end will save that place. It's not the hatred of the coal companies, or anger, but love will save this place.[c]

The words of a rancher can easily be transferred to our awe for the cities we love. Who doesn't gaze from the street and appreciate the hours of sweat and care that went into building and maintaining beloved urban places? Who doesn't ruminate on the thousands of days before, where someone has sat just like you and watched the daily activities unfold? Who doesn't feel a tingle of connection when walking along a well-worn footpath? I believe love will save our places too, if they are indeed loveable.

HOW DO YOU MAKE A PLACE MORE LOVEABLE?

Answering this question has become my raison d'etre - I only take on work that I deem "projects for places we love." So far, what I've found is that it comes down to working together, intervention, and celebration.

The "working together" part has been a key way for me to learn about the human side of city building. The process of working alongside others on something worthwhile or just plain fun has actually created my strongest ties to this city. Working together creates bonds with people and place, and powerful memories of joint accomplishment. It's an investment in relationships and the place you live, but it's also motivation for others.

The trouble is, we often lack venues and opportunities to work together or even be together nowadays. We live in an isolated world and most of our city spaces are in need of an intervention. Great blocks and neighborhoods give people excuses to linger, to volunteer, to ask questions and take part. Even as citizens, without a City Hall paycheck or engineering/planning/architecture degree, we can all create our own interventions or playful additions to our urban habitat. This is the physical side of city-building that communities are rapidly prototyping across the world. Our interventions can reinforce the humanness of our cities and give us reasons and avenues to work together.[ci]

Finally, it's important to celebrate. Like the harvest feasts of yesteryear, we can validate hard work with the act of celebration. Food, drink, art, music, dancing - this is all so much more wonderful when it's well-deserved. A tradition of gratitude for our neighbors, for the places we share, and for the forces and co-existence that nurture them helps to keep the good work flowing.

Our situation is obviously precarious. We've done some serious, perhaps irreversible damage to our climate, ecosystems, finances, and communities. Current levels of inequality are staggering and our political systems are ill-equipped to drive transformation. It can be hard to have any hope at all. But I believe in the places that are loved. I believe that the survival skills we need are gratitude and generosity - caring about each other and our homes enough to learn, adapt, and be resourceful. Humanizing our cities is both a means and an end to doing that. I believe that as long as we're walking that path together, we'll have reason to celebrate.

25. TOO WILD TO IMAGINE
by Charles Marohn

(June 1, 2015) If we had gone to a family living in an American city in 1940 and told them that, in the next decade, they would sell their home for a lot less than it was currently worth and move to a farm field on the far reaches of the city, they would have thought us crazy.

They would have informed us that their current home had been in their family for a couple of generations, that all those little additions had been built by their ancestors. They would have referenced their neighbors, their local church, the schools the kids attended — the ones they had attended — their job, their friends and all of the other complex social connections that bound them to their place. They would have been bewildered at the suggestion that a way of life they knew and understood would change so radically.

Yet, within a decade, move to the farm field is exactly what they did. In droves. And while we can ascribe all sorts of nefarious or ignorant motivations for this mass migration, it is pretty simple to understand if we don't over-think things:

Their current house was a bad investment — it was declining in value in a neighborhood showing outwards signs of decline, all of which was structured around a way of life in decline — while the new home was a good investment.

Everything about that home in the field was shiny, new and exciting. The migration had the power of massive state subsidy behind it, which was also perfectly aligned with the industries of the day. What once seem too wild to imagine became self-evident as more and more people pined for their own space in America's suburbs.

A couple of weeks ago I spoke in Grand Forks, North Dakota. I had the honor of being able to meet with some of the editorial staff at the Grand Forks Herald, an experience I cherished more than the usual editorial board interaction because of the storied history of that great paper. I'm still inspired by the work the Herald did in the 1997 floods — work that won them a Pulitzer prize — when they continued to publish a paper every day, even while the city simultaneously burned and flooded around them.

I also really like Grand Forks. While the edge was epically depressing — superimpose the standard Americana strip development on the vast barrenness of a North Dakota landscape — the downtown was really good, trending to great. There's way more life in downtown Grand Forks on your standard Thursday night than say, in downtown Kansas City. And the people in Grand Forks are seemingly focused on all the right things. The president of their Downtown Development Association — a guy named Jonathan Holth — gave a great speech about their need to use underutilized space, to grow incrementally, to hit lots of singles and avoid the temptation to swing for the fences.[cii] Just perfect.

I had to smile a little bit last week when I was copied on social media with a link to the Herald's editorial that followed my visit.[ciii] I loved it because, while it stopped sort of saying I was wrong, in true North Dakota fashion, it essentially intimated that my arguments failed the plausibility standard. In a less civilized part of the country they may have suggested I was full of human excrement or even said bad things about my parentage. Here's part of that editorial:

> "When you spread out this much over a large area, everything starts to go bad over time," [Marohn] said.
>
> Whoa, now. We asked Marohn if he's advocating contraction. After all, he was in Grand Forks to speak, and we all know our city's footprint is expanding daily. A few new houses probably have sprung up around the new south-side grade school just in the time it took to read this.
>
> We told him we don't see his idea as realistic. And besides, where would one even start?[civ]

These guys were really sharp and caught on to the implications rather quickly. Here is a guy saying there isn't enough money to maintain all this stuff. If something can't be maintained, it won't be. Thus he seems to be saying that we're going to walk away from a lot of stuff we've built. *Whoa, now.*

Being very practical, they asked me how you would even do this. If the city wanted to intentionally contract to something financially viable, how could that even happen? In retrospect, I should have channeled my inner politician (if I even have one) and stayed on message instead of trying to answer what is a massively complex — and ultimately unanswerable — question. Here's why:

> *His answer: Split the city into divisions — for example, downtown, the near-downtown neighborhoods and the outlying area. He said downtown and the core neighborhoods have the potential to be very profitable.*
>
> *But start with downtown, he said: "To me, I don't let a street or sidewalk go bad there, and I would do whatever I can to get small, incremental investments that build on each other throughout those areas. [...] The stuff just on the edge of that, if good investments were made and the neighborhoods expand and mature, they could also function in much the same way.*[cv]

Yeah, that's certainly what I said, although it is not likely to resonate with those not already predisposed to agree. It also leads to the logical next question, which was also covered in the editorial:

> *What about those of us who live beyond those key areas?*
>
> *"If people want to live there, great. But what should be off the table are subsidies (to live there). If you want to pay for that road out there, great. If you don't mind having a dirt road ... that's fine, too," he said. "And we probably cannot afford five-minute fire-protection service out there."*[cvi]

And this is where I think we humans struggle the most. These guys at the Herald are really smart. If they weren't, they would not have written an editorial that, I feel, got right to the heart of the problem: We're not wired to look at things this way. Here's how they honestly address that.

Actually, it's not so much that I disagree with Marohn; it's just difficult to imagine the contraction of services in areas away from a healthy city's core. Among other reasons, Marohn's proposals won't happen because so many decision-makers live in the very places he has declared untenable. It just isn't fathomable.

Downtown Grand Forks is a great place. After all, it's where the Herald decided to rebuild post-flood. And Marohn's approach is interesting, even intriguing.

It's just too wild and far-flung to imagine coming to pass.[cvii]

It's just too wild to imagine. I respect that; he's right. It is wild to imagine that a continent of thoughtful people would throw away thousands of years of knowledge on how to build successful places, embark on a massive social, cultural and financial experiment, take on hordes of debt in the name of growth and then call it all "the normal way things are done." Yet, that's what we did.

It's also wild to imagine it coming to an end, to step back and ponder the ways in which what can't be maintained won't be maintained, what it actually means to correct a mistake made on such a grand scale.

I started out with the story of the 1940's family because we have a precedent here. If Detroit is too uncomfortable for you, or if you have hang-ups that keep you from seeing it as the canary in the coal mine, then envision that pre-war family who could not have imagined the change that was about to overtake them. Suburbanization looks like a *fait-accompli* today, yet it took place in slow motion over a couple of decades, the slow and unsure first steps of the pioneers eventually leading to a mass migration to a living arrangement that seemed like a better investment. That we would follow their lead and eventually abandon places that aren't working — bad investments — should come as no surprise.

Just because something is too wild to imagine doesn't make it too wild to be true. What we don't have the money to maintain, ultimately won't be maintained, whether we want it to or not.

Taking small steps now to make your place a Strong Town is a strategy with huge upside and very limited downside. Let's not make our inability to fully comprehend massive change — a change which cannot be fully comprehended — keep us from doing what is prudent.

GLOSSARY

At Strong Towns, we value transparency, clarity and accessibility. That means we try to avoid jargon as much as possible, but there are a few phrases that crop up in our writing and speaking now and again that we wanted to make sure are clearly defined. Whether you're new to Strong Towns or you've been with us for years, we hope you'll find these definitions to be a helpful reference when reading our work.

Chaotic but Smart: This comes from something called Carlson's Law, an adage from Silicon Valley. Carlson's Law states, "In a world where so many people now have access to education and cheap tools of innovation, innovation that happens from the bottom up tends to be chaotic but smart. Innovation that happens from the top down tends to be orderly but dumb." When we talk about Chaotic but Smart at Strong Towns, we're referring to projects and initiatives that start outside of traditional governmental systems, involve little risk of public funds yet have the potential create significant improvement. In successful places, Chaotic but Smart initiatives find their way into, and tend to reshape, existing bureaucracies.

Desperation Phase: This is the part of the Growth Ponzi Scheme (see below) where local governments, overwhelmed with debt and obligations, are so desperate for growth that they are willing to make any financial deal, regardless of how bad, if it provides even the illusion of progress. This is most often seen towards the end of the second life cycle and the beginning of the third. Such deals often include, but are not limited to: tax subsidies, the creation of shovel-ready sites, subsidized extension of public utilities, land giveaways and more.

Growth Ponzi Scheme: This is the way most local governments finance growth and development. Projects that are supposed to create growth are financed through one of the Mechanisms of Growth with most of the costs of the transaction being paid by someone other than the local government. In return for this "growth," the local government agrees to assume the long term obligation to maintain the infrastructure and provide service to the property. While cash flow may be positive in the early years, the exchange of a near-term cash benefit for a long-term obligation ultimately results in a negative cash flow when the maintenance bill comes due. To address the shortfall, cities pursue additional growth providing them with the short-term cash needed in exchange for more, long-term liabilities. Like any Ponzi scheme, once the rate of growth stops accelerating, the compounding liabilities that come due result in insolvency.

Human Scale: Building at a scale, and with a level of detail and nuance, that creates a sense-of-place for a person on foot.

Illusion of Wealth: The short-term "success" that a local government experiences during the first life cycle of the Growth Ponzi Scheme.

Infrastructure Cult: The chorus of advocacy organizations, media outlets and politicians that reflexively believe that infrastructure spending is a good financial investment.

Life Cycle: The period of time between when a piece of infrastructure is built and when it needs reconstruction or replacement.

Productive Place: A place that creates enough excess wealth to make sustaining its basic infrastructure financially feasible.

Quantum Theory of Economic Development: The assertion frequently put forward by engineers, city planners, economic development professionals and their supporters that, while individual public projects may not make financial sense, the aggregate effect of all the public investments being made are positive, even if they can't be measured.

Road: A high speed connection between two Productive Places.

Street: A platform for creating wealth.

Stroad: A street/road hybrid. A stroad attempts to provide both high speed travel and wealth creation but fails at both, despite the enormous cost. These are not only the lowest returning type of transportation investment, they are also the most dangerous, combining high speeds with complexity. If you are traveling between 25 mph and 50mph, you are almost certainly on a stroad.

Suburban Experiment: The approach to growth and

development that has become dominant in North America during the 20th Century. There are two distinguishing characteristics of this approach that differentiate it from the Traditional Development Pattern. They are: (1) New growth happens at a large scale and (2) Construction is done to a finished state; there is no further growth anticipated after the initial construction.

Traditional Development Pattern: The approach to growth and development that humans used for thousands of years across different cultures, continents and latitudes. There are two distinguishing characteristics of this pattern that differentiate it from the Suburban Experiment. They are: (1) Growth happens incrementally over time and (2) All neighborhoods are on a continuum of improvement.

ABOUT THE AUTHORS

Charles Marohn, PE, AICP

Charles Marohn - known as "Chuck" to friends and colleagues - is a Professional Engineer (PE) licensed in the State of Minnesota and a member of the American Institute of Certified Planners (AICP). Chuck is the Founder and President of Strong Towns. He has a Bachelor's degree in Civil Engineering from the University of Minnesota's Institute of Technology and a Masters in Urban and Regional Planning from the University of Minnesota's Humphrey Institute.

He is the author of *Thoughts on Building Strong Towns (Volume 1)* and *A World Class Transportation System* as well as the host of the Strong Towns Podcast and a primary writer for Strong Towns' web content. He has spoken in dozens of towns and cities across North America, and speaks regularly for diverse audiences and venues.

Chuck grew up on a small farm in Central Minnesota. The oldest of three sons of two elementary school teachers, he graduated from Brainerd High School in 1991. Chuck joined the Minnesota National Guard on his 17th birthday during his junior year of high school and served for nine years. Besides being passionate about building a stronger America, he loves playing music, is an obsessive reader and religiously follows his favorite team, the Minnesota Twins.

Chuck and his wife live with their two daughters and two Samoyeds in his hometown of Brainerd, Minnesota.

Matthias Leyrer

Matthias Leyrer has been a regular contributor to Strong Towns since 2014. He is an aspiring developer and advocate. A designer by trade, he looks to fill the mundanity of the work week by writing about urban planning, land use and transportation at his blog, keycity.co. He is inspired by the idea that every city deserves the chance to be beautiful and that we can build cities and towns worth passing on to the next generation. In addition to writing for his blog, Matthias assists Strong Towns with graphic design, including the creation of our Strong Towns memes (seen throughout this volume).

Nathaniel Hood

Nathaniel Hood has been a regular contributor for Strong Towns since 2011 and was the first person to ever donate money to Strong Towns. He is a founding member of Streets.MN and lives in St. Paul. Nate can be found online at Streets.MN.

Andrew Price

Andrew Price has been a regular contributor to Strong Towns since 2013 and is a founding member of the organization. Andrew is a software developer by day and an urbanist by night. He is passionate about traditional urbanism – he believes in fine-grained, highly walkable places that are built for people. He grew up in Australia and now lives in the United States with his wife. Andrew is a regular contributor on Strong Towns and runs his own blog, andrewalexanderprice.com. Andrew's motivation to be involved in Strong Towns and urbanism is to create a great place that he and his wife, and one day their children and their future generations will want to call home.

Rachel Quednau

Rachel Quednau serves as Communications Specialist for Strong Towns and has been a regular contributor for Strong Towns since 2015. Rachel is a Midwesterner currently living in Milwaukee, WI. Previously, she worked for several organizations fighting to end homelessness at the federal and local levels. She draws from her experiences living in New York City, Washington, DC, Walla Walla, WA and Minneapolis, MN to help her build better places wherever she is. One of Rachel's favorite ways to get to know a new city is by going for a run in it.

Johnny Sanphillippo

Johnny Sanphillippo has been a regular contributor for Strong Towns since 2014. He is an amateur architecture buff with a passionate interest in where and how we all live and occupy the landscape, from small rural towns to skyscrapers and everything in between. He travels often, conducts interviews with people of interest, and gathers photos and video of places worth talking about. Johnny writes for Strong Towns, and his blog, GranolaShotgun.com.

Daniel Herriges

Daniel Herriges has been a regular contributor to Strong Towns since 2015 and is a founding member of the organization. Daniel is a Master's student in Urban and Regional Planning at the University of Minnesota. His obsession with maps began before he could read. His budding environmentalism can be traced back to age 4, when he yelled at his parents for stepping on weeds growing in sidewalk cracks. His love of great urban design and human-scaled, livable places has also been lifelong. Daniel has a B.A. from Stanford University in Human Biology with a concentration in Conservation and Sustainable Development. After college, he worked as an environmental activist for several years, in support of indigenous people's rights and conservation in the Amazon rainforest. He can often be found hiking or cycling. Daniel is from St. Paul, Minnesota.

Gracen Johnson

Gracen Johnson has been a regular contributor for Strong Towns since 2014 and is a founding member of the organization. She calls her work, "Projects for Places we Love." She mostly helps individuals and organizations with strategy, research, communications, and outreach. Despite finishing her MPhil in Planning, Growth, and Regeneration in 2013, she has never stopped studying the city. Gracen thinks of her day-to-day as action research, diving into the question of how Strong Citizenship can transform a place. She lives with her partner in the The Maritimes region of Canada. In addition to her regular writing for the Strong Towns website, Gracen has also created (and continues to create) many of Strong Towns' short films. You can find her online at GracenJohnson.com.

Michael "Mike" McGinn

Mike McGinn was Mayor of Seattle from 2010-2013. Before becoming mayor, he started and ran a non-profit, Great City, that focused on urban sustainability and built on his experiences as a long time neighborhood and environmental volunteer. Mike continues to work on causes he cares about, as well as hosting a podcast called *You, Me, Us, Now*, that profiles the work of "people trying to change things."

ABOUT STRONG TOWNS

Strong Towns is a national media organization whose mission is to advocate for a model of development that allows America's cities, towns and neighborhoods to grow financially strong and resilient.

For the United States to be a prosperous country, it must have strong cities, towns and neighborhoods. Enduring prosperity for our communities cannot be artificially created from the outside but must be built from within, incrementally over time. A Strong Towns approach relies on incremental investments instead of large, transformative projects, emphasizes resiliency of result over efficiency of execution, and is inspired by bottom-up action, not top-down systems.

Strong Towns produces award-winning daily articles and podcasts, as well as events across the country. Strong Towns has thousands of members throughout the world.

Learn more at www.StrongTowns.org.

Endnotes

[i] See http://www.strongtowns.org/journal/2011/12/12/best-of-blog-asce-and-the-infrastructure-cult.html

[ii] See http://www.strongtowns.org/journal/2014/7/24/some-perspective-on-the-gas-tax.html

[iii] See http://www.strongtowns.org/confessions

[iv] See http://www.strongtowns.org/journal/2015/1/28/a-true-complete-street

[v] See http://www.strongtowns.org/journal/2014/7/2/follow-the-money.html

[vi] Read more on the Growth Ponzi Scheme http://www.strongtowns.org/the-growth-ponzi-scheme/

[vii] Watch the video at https://www.youtube.com/watch?v=P9BUyWVg1xI

[viii] Condon, Patrick and Janet Moore. "Minnesota's broken bridges, ruined roads: All agree something must be done." *Star Tribune,* January 4, 2015. Accessed March 8, 2016. http://www.startribune.com/broken-bridges-ruined-roads-all-agree-something-must-be-done/287421581/?c=y&page=2

[ix] Ibid.

[x] See http://t4america.org/docs/bridgereport2013/2013BridgeReport.pdf

[xi] See http://www.strongtowns.org/journal/2011/10/24/dig-baby-dig.html

[xii] See http://www.dot.state.mn.us/stcroixcrossing/background.html

[xiii] See https://www.youtube.com/watch?v=GO2P9h-wPVI

[xiv] Condon, Patrick. "Minnesota's broken bridges."

[xv] Ibid.

[xvi] See http://blog.tstc.org/2015/10/15/fedup-with-congestion-senator-murphy-seeks-to-solve-connecticuts-commuting-problems/

[xvii] See https://www.fhwa.dot.gov/ohim/onh00/chart3.htm

[xviii] See http://www.strongtowns.org/journal/2014/7/24/some-perspective-on-the-gas-tax.html

[xix] See http://www.strongtowns.org/journal/2012/10/23/embracing-congestion.html

[xx] *Friday Roundtable*. "Transportation during the 2015 session." Hosted by Kerri Miller. Minnesota Public Radio, January 16, 2015. Accessed on March 8, 2016. http://www.mprnews.org/story/2015/01/16/daily-circuit-friday-roundtable

[xxi] Ibid.

[xxii] See http://www.strongtowns.org/journal/2009/8/13/the-reality-of-brainerds-parkway.html

[xxiii] See http://www.transportationalliance.com/content/please-thank-our-alliance-sponsors

[xxiv] See http://www.strongtowns.org/journal/2014/7/24/some-perspective-on-the-gas-tax.html

[xxv] See http://www.strongtowns.org/journal/2015/1/7/americas-suburban-experiment

[xxvi] Miller, Kerri. Transportation.

[xxvii] Trombino, Paul. Presentation for the Urban Land Institute – Iowa Chapter, Des Moines, IA, June 30, 2015.

[xxviii] Ibid.

[xxix] http://www.census.gov/compendia/statab/2012/tables/12s1089.pdf

[xxx] Nelson, Emma. "As maintenance costs rise, homeowners ask cities to take over private streets." *Star Tribune,* October 31, 2015. Accessed on March 8, 2016. http://www.startribune.com/as-maintenance-costs-rise-homeowners-ask-cities-to-take-over-private-streets/339131001/?section=%2F

[xxxi] Ibid.

[xxxii] See http://www.strongtowns.org/journal/2014/8/19/is-a-street-an-asset.html

[xxxiii] Nelson, Emma. Maintenance costs.

[xxxiv] See http://www.strongtowns.org/journal/2012/4/2/assessing-our-future.html

[xxxv] See https://www.youtube.com/watch?v=eIvqSz048U8

[xxxvi] http://mutcd.fhwa.dot.gov/htm/2009/part1/part1a.htm

[xxxvii] http://www.collectorsweekly.com/articles/murder-machines/

[xxxviii] Ibid.

[xxxix] Ibid.

[xl] Clukey, Keshia and Paul Grondahl. "Boy killed while crossing the street." *Times Union*, February 13, 2013. Accessed on March 8, 2016. http://www.timesunion.com/news/article/Child-hit-by-garbage-truck-in-Albany-6077250.php#photo-7516889

[xli] Ibid.

[xlii] Ibid.

[xliii] Google search. Accessed on March 8, 2016 https://www.google.com/search?q=definition+of+accident&oq=definition+of+accident&aqs=chrome..69i57j0l5.5143j0j7&sourceid=chrome&es_sm=93&ie=UTF-8

[xliv] Clukey, Keshia. "Boy Killed."

[xlv] See https://www.google.com/maps/@42.6653443,-73.7735497,3a,75y,35.76h,77.87t/data=!3m6!1e1!3m4!1smMK79FILZoeKULYvycqNzw!2e0!7i13312!8i6656

[xlvi] Ibid.

[xlvii] Ibid

[xlviii] See http://www.washingtonpost.com/news/wonkblog/wp/2015/04/17/why-one-way-streets-really-are-the-worst/

[xlix] Jaffe, Eric. "The Case Against One-Way Streets. *CityLab*, January 31, 2013. Accessed March 8, 2016 http://www.citylab.com/commute/2013/01/case-against-one-way-streets/4549/

[l] See http://www.strongtowns.org/journal/2014/12/3/just-another-pedestrian-killed

[li] See http://www.masslive.com/news/index.ssf/2015/12/protesters_decry_continuing_ha.html

[lii] Schneider, Avery. "Child dead after vehicle accident in Delaware Park." *WBFO 88.7*, May 30, 2015. Accessed March 8, 2016.

[liii] Cuomo, Andrew. "Governor Cuomo Orders Speed Limit Lowered on Portion of Scajaquada Expressway," *Governor.NY.gov.* May 31, 2015. Accessed March 8, 2016.
https://www.governor.ny.gov/news/governor-cuomo-orders-speed-limit-lowered-portion-scajaquada-expressway

http://news.wbfo.org/post/child-dead-after-vehicle-accident-delaware-park

[liv] "Child dies after car crashes into day care on Goldenrod Road." *WFTV,* April 10, 2014. Accessed March 8, 2016.
http://www.wftv.com/news/news/local/children-hurt-when-car-crashes-kindercare-goldenro/nfWrR/

[lv] See https://www.google.com/maps/place/Goldenrod+Road+KinderCare/@28.598181,-81.286512,240m/data=!3m1!1e3!4m2!3m1!1s0x0:0x3e7e9853a218182c!6m1!1e1

[lvi] Breen, David. "After fatal day care crash, Orange looks at safeguards." *Orlando Sentinel,* February 9, 2015. Accessed March 8, 2016.
http://www.orlandosentinel.com/news/breaking-news/os-orange-crash-protection-daycare-20150209-story.html

[lvii] Ibid.

[lviii] Ibid.

[lix] New Staff. "Police: Witnesses say driver ran red light before hitting, killing 3 kids." *KVAL,* February 21, 2015. Accessed March 15, 2016.
http://kval.com/news/local/police-witnesses-say-driver-ran-red-light-before-hitting-killing-3-kids

[lx] See https://www.google.com/maps/place/Main+St+%26+N+54th+St,+Springfield,+OR+97478/@44.045688,-122.935147,17z/data=!4m2!3m1!1s0x54c0e0a4ce5e5653:0x83a07a62fe73fc4b

[lxi] Springfield's ideas after 3 kids die in crosswalk." *Associated Press,* March 8, 2015. Accessed March 15, 2016.
http://koin.com/2015/03/08/springfields-ideas-after-3-kids-die-in-crosswalk/

[lxii] Hill, Christian. "Kids' deaths spur safety proposals." *Register Guard,*

[lxiii] Ibid.

[lxiv] The Oregonian Editorial Board. "When a tragic accident is just a tragic accident: Editorial." *The Oregonian,* May 9, 2015. Accessed March 15, 2015
http://www.oregonlive.com/opinion/index.ssf/2015/05/when_a_tragic_accident_is_just.html

[lxv] Ibid.

[lxvi] Ibid.

[lxvii] See https://www.google.com/maps/@40.7409055,-74.0016807,3a,75y,102.23h,74t/data=!3m6!1e1!3m4!1sbR2KCjyWihXou-jhRMdwiQ!2e0!7i13312!8i6656

[lxviii] See https://www.google.com/maps/place/200+W+Main+St,+Carmel,+IN+460 32/@39.9783461,-86.1297669,3a,75y,34.05h,76.74t/data=!3m7!1e1!3m5!1sfGUsO4uIw1EP bcSzR_PCBQ!2e0!6s%2F%2Fgeo2.ggpht.com%2Fcbk%3Fpanoid%3DfG UsO4uIw1EPbcSzR_PCBQ%26output%3Dthumbnail%26cb_client%3D maps_sv.tactile.gps%26thumb%3D2%26w%3D203%26h%3D100%26ya w%3D166.49651%26pitch%3D0!7i13312!8i6656!4m2!3m1!1s0x8814ad b5f8976231:0x6b3881ff75fb31d0

[lxix] See http://www.andrewalexanderprice.com/blog20121015.php

[lxx] See http://www.andrewalexanderprice.com/blog20140422.php

[lxxi] See http://www.andrewalexanderprice.com/blog20150916.php

[lxxii] See http://www.andrewalexanderprice.com/blog20150914.php

[lxxiii] National Alliance to End Homelessness. *The State of Homelessness in America in 2014.* May 2014. Accessed March 15, 2016.
http://www.endhomelessness.org/library/entry/the-state-of-homelessness-2014

[lxxiv] Read more at https://www.ideals.illinois.edu/bitstream/handle/2142/31069/Miller_Abbilyn.pdf?sequence=1

[lxxv] Read more at http://occupymadisoninc.com/

[lxxvi] Read more at http://www.archdaily.com/324418/adapt-nyc-competition-announces-micro-apartment-winner-and-finalists/

[lxxvii] See the full thread at https://www.reddit.com/r/engineering/comments/398dbk/nonprofit_cl aims_engineers_show_conscious/?sort=old&limit=500

[lxxviii] Leslie, Jacques. "The Trouble with Megaprojects." *The New Yorker*, April 11, 2015. Accessed March 15, 2016 http://www.newyorker.com/news/news-desk/bertha-seattle-infrastructure-trouble-megaprojects

[lxxix] Ibid.

[lxxx] Ibid.

[lxxxi] Ibid.

[lxxxii] Ibid.

[lxxxiii] Ibid.

[lxxxiv] See https://www.google.com/maps/@39.107005,-84.4868155,1316m/data=!3m1!1e3

[lxxxv] Lehman, Joseph. "'The Overton Window': Made in Michigan." *Mackinac Center for Public Policy*, July 5, 2010. Accessed March 15, 2016 http://www.mackinac.org/13075

[lxxxvi] See the video at http://www.humantransit.org/2015/07/one-of-my-best-presentations-ever-.html

[lxxxvii] Bolotsky, Josh. "Use your radical fringe to shift the Overton window." *Beautiful Trouble*. Accessed March 15, 2016. http://beautifultrouble.org/principle/use-your-radical-fringe-to-shift-the-overton-window/

[lxxxviii] See http://ecode360.com/15238455

[lxxxix] Schmidt, Margaret. "Sinatra Drive in Hoboken to become pedestrian mall on Sundays." *NJ.com*. June 8, 2010. Accessed March 15, 2016. http://www.nj.com/hobokennow/index.ssf/2010/06/sinatra_drive_in_hoboken_to_cl.html

[xc] See http://www.hobokennj.org/departments/transportation-parking/surrenderyourpermit/

[xci] See http://www.hobokennj.org/departments/transportation-

parking/parking/

[xcii] "Site Design, Parking and Zoning for Shopping Centers." *American Planning Association*, January 1959. Accessed March 16, 2016. https://www.planning.org/pas/at60/report59.htm

[xciii] See http://homes.trovit.com/269057/hoboken-price-rent-property

[xciv] See http://www.nj.com/hudson/index.ssf/2014/10/hundreds_wait_on_line_for_chance_at_low-income_housing_in_hoboken_and_weehawken.html

[xcv] Wymeren, Adam. "The cost of parking In U.S. cities." *Fox News*, February 12, 2012. Accessed March 16, 2016. http://www.foxnews.com/leisure/2012/02/21/cost-parking-in-us-cities/

[xcvi] See http://www.nj.com/hudson/index.ssf/2013/11/hoboken_scored_most_walkable_city_in_the_country.html

[xcvii] See http://www.strongtowns.org/journal/2015/11/18/a-map-of-cities-that-got-rid-of-parking-minimums

[xcviii] "Hermann Goering." *Wikiquote*. Accessed March 15, 2016. https://en.wikiquote.org/wiki/Hermann_Göring

[xcix] For years I (Chuck Marohn) did zoning work in recreational communities across Minnesota. I ran into countless faux environmentalists who were completely comfortable with their own home on the lake but felt the next person in was going irreparably damage the natural environment.

[c] Klein, Naomi. *This Changes Everything: Capitalism vs. The Climate*. New York: Simon & Schuster, 2015.

[ci] See http://gracenjohnson.com/index.php#portfolio

[cii] Watch the speech at https://youtu.be/gRxpXWoG7RA?t=21m

[ciii] Wenzel, Korrie. "To stop sprawl, should Grand Forks deliberately contract?" *Grand Forks Herald*. May 20, 2015. Accessed March 15, 2016. http://www.grandforksherald.com/opinion/featured-columnists/3748705-korrie-wenzel-stop-sprawl-should-grand-forks-deliberately

[civ] Ibid.

[cv] Wenzel, Korrie. "Sprawl."

[cvi] Ibid.
[cvii] Ibid.

Made in the USA
Middletown, DE
30 September 2016